Conversations With Top Real Estate Investors Vol. 3

With contributing Authors

Bob Snyder

Jay & Nancy Abramovitz

Robert E. Asercion

Benjamin Octavio Gallego III

Robin Haley

John Harmon

Patrick & Paul McCrimmon

Dr. Chau Ong

Valerie M. Sargent

Richard Stock

Joshua White

Marsha Yearian

Munira Zahabi

Woody Woodward

D.U. Publishing
www.dupublishing.com

Warning—Disclaimer

The purpose of this book is to educate and inspire. This book is not intended to give advice or make promises or guarantees that anyone following the ideas, tips, suggestions, techniques or strategies will have the same results as the people listed throughout the stories contained herein. The author, publisher and distributor(s) shall have neither liability nor responsibility to anyone with respect to any loss or damage caused, or alleged to be caused, directly or indirectly by the information contained in this book.

ISBN: 978-0-9982340-6-9

Table of Contents

Introduction..i

Bob Snyder 1

Jay & Nancy Abramovitz..19

Robert E. Asercion...37

Benjamin Octavio Gallego III.......................................55

Robin Haley..65

John Harmon..76

Patrick & Paul McCrimmon...93

Dr. Chau Ong..113

Valerie M. Sargent..125

Richard Stock 141

Joshua White 150

Marsha Yearian...162

Munira Zahabi 176

Woody Woodward 191

Introduction

Have you ever wanted to be sitting at the table when major real estate transactions were happening just to be able to glean insider information? If your answer was, "Yes" then this book is dedicated to you. You are going to be like a fly on the wall as top real estate investors are being interviewed and sharing their tips and strategies to being successful. These are honest and raw interviews with the intent to inspire you to follow your real estate dreams.

Bob Snyder

Renatus was founded and is led by 25-year entrepreneur, Mr. Bob Snyder. As CEO and President, Mr. Snyder is responsible for day-to-day company operations, affiliate marketing program expansion, course curriculum evaluation and renewal, practitioner-instructor recruiting, and month-over-month increased sales performance.

Mr. Snyder began his entrepreneurial journey over 25 years ago with the desire to leave a positive mark on the world. Establishing himself as a marketing leader, he gained first-hand knowledge of what drives marketing and team-building success. Mr. Snyder built and managed sales organizations with tens of thousands of individuals, achieved top status in multiple companies, and became a top income earner in the direct selling industry. He has freely shared his formula for success as he served on more than a dozen leadership counsels and advisory boards in the direct sales industry, received recognition in national publications as an expert in his field and has personally mentored over a dozen marketers to become seven-figure earners.

After years of building and growing marketing teams, Mr. Snyder's vision transitioned him into developing companies to expand the entrepreneurial spirit that has made this country the world's economic leader. He has founded and co-founded dozens of companies that have collectively produced hundreds of millions of dollars in revenue. His real estate company completed over 2,500 real estate transactions while his former education company trained over 60,000 entrepreneurs on the subject of real estate investing and business ownership.

Contact Info:

www.MyRenatus.com

Shannon:

According to Forbes magazine, real estate is one of the top three ways that people become wealthy. As a real estate expert, why do you feel that this is the case?

Bob:

Because real estate is one of the three basic human needs: food, water, and shelter. There's always going to be a demand for real estate. Tech companies come and go, financial companies come and go, media companies come and go, but real estate is constant, and we are always going to have a need for it. Those individuals who position themselves with the right kind of properties are always going to be able to generate monthly cash flow.

Shannon:

Is that what inspired you to get into real estate: supply and demand?

Bob:

No. What inspired me to get into real estate was my wife. She dragged me kicking and screaming into real estate.

Here's the thing, I didn't understand it, and we always fear what we don't understand. I had been raised with the idea that a secure retirement required investments in the stock market. The problem was that I kept giving money to my broker and I continued to GET broker!

My wife was increasingly frustrated that we kept losing money on Wall Street, even from our conservative mutual fund investments. They weren't producing any kind of a sustainable return. By contrast, her mother and father invested in real estate while she was growing up. They made a habit of buying properties, paying them off, selling them, and buying others to build their portfolios. They developed cash flows that would take care of them in their retirement. Today, my father-in-law is eighty-eight years old and he and his wife live very comfortably from their paid-for real estate. The proof's in the pudding.

So, after losing a bunch of money on Wall Street my wife came to me and said, "Listen. We need to be in real estate. It's the way to build and secure our future and our kids' future. It's not Wall Street. It's not the stock market and it's not this other nonsense that you've been dealing with." Unfortunately, I was stubborn. I did not want to listen to her, but she was right and the last thing in the world I ever wanted was to tell her that she was right.

Shannon:
Now, looking back, you think, "Thank Goodness she was right."

Bob:
Yes, and think about what happened as a result of that, but it didn't happen overnight. She worked on me and worked on me, and I kept saying no. Then she finally came to me and she said, "Listen, Bob. I found this great little duplex. Its owner occupied on one side with a tenant on the other side, so the owner really fixed it up nice. The property is for sale by owner. We can get it a decent deal. It'll cash flow after we get a mortgage on it. You won't have to deal with it. I will manage it. I just need your support because if I don't do this I'm going to regret this rest of my life and you wouldn't want that, would you?" I mean, come on, what do you say to that?

Shannon:
You say, "You know, honey, I think we should get into real estate."

Bob:
I said, "You're absolutely right, but if this thing goes south I don't know if I'll be able to resist saying I told you so."

About a year later we were taking a look at the property's rents and depreciation schedule. All I could think was, "Holy smokes, we've got somebody living in our investment property who works all month long to make sure that we're the first one that gets paid. What an amazing business model." Then we get all these tax write offs, and the property was appreciating in value. This is phenomenal! It was one of those moments where I was like, "Wow, I'm glad I thought of it."

Shannon:

So when you were sitting in that real estate office, did she turn to you and say, "I told you so," or did she just say, "Bob, I am so glad you thought of this."

Bob:

You know, it's funny, Holly was really good about it. She just said, "You know what? You just needed to see it. You just needed to see it and do it," and she was right. All I could think to say was that we need to be doing a whole heck of a lot more of this, and that's what started our real estate investing career.

Back then we were so green, so naïve, we didn't understand real estate. We didn't understand wholesale buying opportunities. We did what 99.9 percent of the investors in this country do: go out, find a property, pay almost full price for it, put a tenant in the darn thing, and then you pray and hope that it's going to cash flow sometime in the next ten years. That's where our investing career started, but it gave me the bug and I had a desire to learn more, to grow in that business, to learn creative real estate strategies so that I could acquire properties for pennies on the dollar or buy them without any money out of pocket. I understood that with the right knowledge and drive to be a successful investor, I would never have to worry about money again.

Shannon:

Now, you've got all this knowledge and you've got years of experience, if someone wanted to get started in real estate, what would you recommend is the very first thing they do?

Bob:

The very first thing they need to do is get educated. That's just it. It's a business whereby if you know what you're doing you can make a whole lot of money and if you don't you can lose a whole lot of money. There is absolutely no ceiling on your income—the sky's the limits. You can become a millionaire, a billionaire, and I'm sure that down the road there will even be trillionaire real estate investors. The problem is, there's no floor either.

Shannon:

Yeah, I guess, if there's no ceiling...

Bob:

Yeah, if you don't know what you're doing, you can lose money. That's the biggest thing. You've got to get educated so that you have at least a common baseline of information, so you know how to fall in love with the deal and not the property. You need to know how to work the numbers and ensure that you are making a good, prudent business decision that's going to be profitable for you. The next thing is you've got to take action. I see too many individuals who fall into the category of what I call, educated derelicts. They're so versed on all sorts of different real estate strategies and different ideas, but they don't do anything with it. It's just fear that holds them back.

Shannon:

What do you do to get over that fear?

Bob:

Again, get educated. Education builds competency and when you feel competent about something you are more likely to take action. Action helps you to overcome fear, so the real formula for success is for a person to get educated and then to get busy. Education without action will not produce results.

For example, there are three types of students: the drop outs, the graduates, and the eternal. Those who keep learning and never start applying what they have learned continue to make up a larger and larger segment of our population. They are paralyzed by fear.

Let me give you an old acronym for fear

False

Evidence

Appearing

Real.

I believe that wealth is a mindset. Individuals start a conversation in their own mind that leads them to a certain belief, that belief either prevents them from moving forward or actually compels them to move forward. How they see risk plays an important role. Somewhere in their internal dialogue is a conversation about risk. When their focus shifts to all that can go wrong with an opportunity, they talk themselves out of moving forward with that opportunity.

That's why we build local communities of real estate investors all across the country. These local groups get together on a regular basis to talk about their real estate deals and what's going on in their business. When you've got somebody brand new who is fearful about fixing and flipping or building cash flow, it makes all the difference in the world to immerse them in an active community of investors. Surrounded by investors who are making offers, doing deals, and making money, a student gains confidence to make it happen for themselves.

At Renatus, we surround our students with examples of success so that they can get a realistic view of what it takes to succeed. In colleges and universities, students are stuck on the degree treadmill. They risk nothing and just keep going from class to class to class and degree to degree to degree. The lack of real world experience is the challenge with higher education.

Shannon:

Which becomes their new job.

Bob:

Yeah. It's not until they get into the real world that they start to experience anything. Believe me, I am a big proponent of education in whatever form that it can possibly come from. Unfortunately, higher education is letting more people down. They're getting degrees in fields of study that they will never make a living in and sometimes it enables them to just stay in that "safe" environment where they never take action which is why student loan debt continues to increase and student outcomes continue to decrease.

Shannon:

So, how do you change that?

Bob:

Specialized knowledge. It's unfortunate that the world of academia will never accept our type of educators because many of them don't have a college degree. Heck, some of them barely got their GED, but they are all successful, profitable investors. As for me, I got right into the world of business and by the time my friends were all graduating from college, I was making two to three times the money they were making.

Shannon:

How did you get educated? What did you do?

Bob:

You're going to love this story. I started my career in sales and marketing and then because of the frustration I dealt with working for someone else, I stepped into the wonderful world of owning and operating my own businesses. I had learned over the years how to build training platforms. I knew how to build sales teams. I knew how to create and build companies and I had a business partner who was also a seasoned entrepreneur. Together we were involved in a travel company but, after 9/11, nobody wanted to talk about travel; everybody was hunkered down and fearful of getting around the world. Our travel business really tanked. I did about everything I possibly could to get the wings back on the plane and make that thing fly again, but it just wasn't happening.

It was at that point that I had a conversation with my partner. I said, "Listen. Sometimes the best way to protect an opportunity is to create a new one." We owned real estate but we didn't understand wholesale buying or a lot about the real estate industry. I suggested we create an educational company centered on real estate investing. Then we hired the big gurus to come in and teach our people how to invest. The idea was that while our students learned, we would learn. What an idea, right?

That's where it all started. But the challenge was that the gurus we hired to teach students, students who paid good money to be in those classes, often refused to teach! They only wanted to whet the appetite of the listener so that they could up sell them to their own courses.

Shannon:

Oh, wow.

Bob:

So I talked to a friend of mine who had a PhD in Education. I told him we had a problem we needed to get beyond. Somehow we had to create a true learning environment instead of the ridiculous circus sales environment that our competitors used. He said he could help and we hired him.

He worked with us, and our staff, very closely for about a year. We brought in subject matter experts (SMEs) to help us take a good look at the real estate industry and construct our curriculum. We went out and organized focus groups from those who had paid money to gurus, both those who had and had not invested yet. All those focus groups assisted us in understanding what holds people back from investing.

We found there were four principle reasons for not investing: I don't have the time, I don't have the money/credit, I don't have the knowledge, or I'm just afraid. Those were the most common excuses. I view them as the excuses that cause failure.

Shannon:

I think we can say that for every aspect of our lives.

Bob:

Yes, we can. As soon as you start doing something, all of a sudden you say, "Hey, that wasn't so bad." I liken it to people who are W-2 employees. Most are fearful about whatever new thing they take on in life. For example, let's go back to the first day they started a new job or a new career. Were they a little intimidated? Were they a little nervous? If they're honest, they're always going to say yes. Fast forward six months. By then they have a pretty good handle on it. Most would say that they had gotten really good at their job and feel confident in it. The challenge is that they rarely ever feel like they are getting paid what they are worth?

We all go through that process. Fear is overcome through action.

We've got to get people in an environment that helps them to take one step after another. That's another thing I learned from Dr. Paul Ripicke. He taught us about the Instructional System design (ISD) methodology for curriculum building. It's what every major college and university in the country uses to build their curriculum paths and focus on student outcomes.

We thought, "well, if Harvard and Yale and Princeton are using this, we can use it too," so we went out and worked with individuals who were actual full-time investors in a specific strategy and we brought them on board. We worked with them to help us craft these classes, and then we taught them how to teach, and then we fired all the gurus. From that point forward, we had real-life investors standing up in front of our classrooms teaching our students. We forbid any of those instructors to ever sell anything in class because we knew that that would be a massive conflict of interest because the minute they started selling they would stop teaching.

Shannon:
Was there one type of person or personality that seemed to be most drawn to your classes or had the type of personality to be the most successful?

Bob:
It's not the personality, it's the circumstance. That's the one thing that all of our students shared; there was a heightened level of dissatisfaction with where they were. It didn't matter whether they were in a successful profession or they were just out of college struggling to make ends meet. They all had a level of dissatisfaction, whether it was enough time with their family, or a good enough future, or they were just sick and tired of working for a boss that didn't appreciate them. They all had a level of dissatisfaction. Again, wealth is a mindset. We just needed to give them hope.

Even for the staff who work here at Renatus, there's a huge shift in their mental framework. They may come in believing they need to contribute each month to their 401(k), but they end up learning how to do creative real estate investing to build their own wealth that they can control. It's pretty exciting to see that the staff members are also embracing the classes and getting out and doing their own deals.

Shannon:
It's kind of exciting because your employees could turn into full-time real estate investors and then you get to hire new employees and teach them, wouldn't you think?

Bob:
You know, there's always that thought in the back of your mind that, key people are going to start making so much money they're going to leave you. I encourage it, but over and over and over again I've got that same group of people who say, "You know what? This is what I want to do for the rest of my life," Renatus is a cause more than it is a job to them because they see the benefits that are showing up in other people's lives and that gives them a great deal of self-satisfaction.

Shannon:
Do you think students should find one real estate investing strategy and stick with that and become an expert, or do you think they should diversify?

Bob:
One of our favorite classes is understanding your investor ID because everybody's different. For example, some individuals have no problem going out there and buying property that they're going to put lower-income tenants into. They're just happy to get that check from the government every single month. Other individuals believe that if they wouldn't live in it, then they won't own it. We have different types of personalities and mindsets. They can all make money in real estate.

What we've got to do is figure out what their investor ID is: do they want quick turn real estate for lump sum cash returns or do they want to build cash flow over time with a nice, passive income from the property? I always tell people, once you figure out your investor ID, then you learn everything you possibly can about that strategy and you focus on that to become an expert.

But, you never stay stuck with just one strategy because markets shift and change. That's why we teach so many different strategies in Renatus. No matter what is happening with the market, no matter what is happening with the economy, if there's a shift or an adjustment in the real estate business and you haven't secured yourself with an understanding of different ways to get the same thing done, you're going to find yourself on the outside looking in and saying, "Well, gee, the economy's bad, so, the opportunity's gone." Not true, my educated students crushed it through the Great Recession. They made money hand over fist while everybody else was bellyaching and moaning that there wasn't an opportunity out there.

Shannon:

Do you have personally a favorite acquisition strategy? Which strategy just makes you the most excited?

Bob:

You know what, I love subject to, but this strategy died during the recession because equity went away and home owners owed more than the property was worth. When I started Renatus, over five years ago, I created a three-hour training series called "Fast Track to Financial Freedom." I showed individuals exactly what was going on in the marketplace, how they could capitalize on what was taking place at that time with real estate investing, and shared with them that we were about 5.2 million homes short of where we needed to be as a nation just to maintain the demand of housing for the increased population.

Many builders do not build in a recession; some went out of business and would need to ramp back up. This would not be an immediate fix. By the time you find raw land, go through all the entitlements, sometimes dealing with the city, and put a foundation in and start putting sticks up to frame the house, you're eighteen to twenty-four months out. It's not like this is just an immediate fix. You don't go, "Oh, there's a demand. I think I'll build a house here." It's going to take a while. I believed that once we got to the backside of the recession, there would be a great housing shortage and that housing shortage would create a massive adjustment in appreciation.

The good news is that the subject to real estate market has come back as prices have increased; we've seen a wild swing. Subject to is a great strategy because it's one of the best ways to acquire multiple properties and not be limited by banks and financial institutions. If you're dependent on conventional lending, you're going to be very, very limited in the amount of real estate you can do and the types of real estate transactions you can do. That's why I love a subject to–it's a great no money down strategy.

Shannon:
What about seller financing? If you're not relying on the banks, are seller financing and subject to the same thing?

Bob:
Well, yes and no. Some might refer to it as another form of seller financing because you are keeping the existing mortgage in place. Generally, seller financing is when a homeowner has a large equity position and they have the ability to create terms for the buyer to make the purchase.

Subject to is when you get the deed to the property, and you become the owner. It's yours. You own it subject to the existing mortgage, but the mortgage still stays in the name of the seller and they stay on the mortgage while you now own and control the home. Now, obviously, you've got to make sure that those payments are made, otherwise the lender will foreclose on the home and even though you're the new owner, they'll take it away from you just like they would have taken it away from the previous owner.

Shannon:
Is a subject to extremely risky as opposed to a standard seller finance, or are they about the same?

Bob:
Oh, no. When we discuss risk we have to think of who's at risk? The seller or the buyer? Individuals looking at selling their home using a subject to' are really in some serious financial stress and they know

that a foreclosure on their credit rating weighs heavier against them than bankruptcy.

Individuals that are stuck in that kind of a situation want to solve that problem before that property goes to auction and the foreclosure is complete. A smart investor will reinstate the loan and purchase the property subject to the existing mortgage. That way, a subject to helps the seller get back on track as far as reestablishing their credit, and it just takes a huge weight off of them. All the stress, all the burden, all the phone calls, all the challenges. It just takes it away so they can get a fresh start and go out and do their thing. The downside for the seller is what happens if the investor who bought the property doesn't make the mortgage payments.

Shannon:
That was my next question.

Bob:
Yep. What happens? Is there a risk? Well, absolutely there's a risk because then that seller could find themselves right back in foreclosure again. Of course, it's no different than the mess they were in to begin with so they're kind of back in the same position. But the bottom line is no investor that is really worth their salt is going to buy a property, put money into that property, and then lose that property because they aren't willing to make the payments. There's a level of assurance that everything's going to happen the way that it should happen.

Now as to the risk to the investor, it's pretty small. Worst case scenario you just walk away from the deal or give it back to the original seller and, if you haven't put any improvements into the property, you're not out anything. If you had put improvements in the property and for some reason you don't have the money to make those monthly mortgage payments, well, then shame on you, you're going to lose the money that you put into the property. Of course, an educated investor would just rent the dang thing out. Then you get a tenant making the mortgage payments for you. There's always a way if you know what you're doing.

Shannon:

That feeds back to all the different strategies. If I, as an investor, were to be in a tough spot and I had learned everything I could learn from you, it seems like I could go to my investment group and say, "Hey, who wants this property? I need help," and they would have the knowledge to help me out.

Bob:

Yep. Absolutely. You know it's just nice to have people that have been there, done that, to be able to pick their brain and lean on them from time to time. We've developed a really unique culture inside of Renatus. It's a culture of servant leadership, meaning that you never, ever ask anybody to do something you wouldn't be willing to do yourself.

If somebody in the community needs help and assistance then we have a pay it forward kind of mentality; but what I see from an awful lot of real estate groups out there, especially a lot of real estate groups, is that they're very motivated to try and maximize their relationships inside the club. There's so many investors in those things that are just looking to prey on brand new investors. They tell them they have a fantastic property that they could turn around and rehab and sell and make 50 grand, but they have to hand over a $10,000 assignment fee to get it.

Then, the brand new greenie goes and buys the property because some seasoned guy said it was going to be a great deal, and they find out that the price they bought it for was over-inflated, the supposed selling price was also over-inflated, and now they're going to lose money on the deal because they didn't know how to work the numbers for themselves. In our community, we apply a lot of emphasis on our leaders and on others in the company to make sure that we take care of community members because they're going to be with us for life.

With that continued emphasis, I outline for them how a deal should be done: Do not sell property to people in the community, unless we want to become a business partner with them, form an LLC with an operating agreement, and have exit strategies already spelled out; do not loan money to anybody in the community or borrow money from anybody in the community unless you become business partners, again with an operating agreement.

That helps to minimize risk. I hate organizations whereby brand new, especially green or naïve individuals get taken advantage of because they think that somebody is trustworthy. You must do your own due diligence because no one is going to care about your financial wellbeing as much as you.

Shannon:

You know, that is so unique to your organization and I love it. If more people just lived their life that way, not just in real estate but just lived their life that way, our world would be so incredibly different.

Bob:

We are all about student outcomes. When somebody buys an educational package from us, after the first year, if they're in good standing with the company, we convert them over to complimentary lifetime access. That means that they're going to have access to refreshed or improved and updated classes given to them for free, for life.

If we have new classes and new material that we roll out to the field, we just give it to our students, again without any additional charge. The complimentary lifetime access is a very, very coveted feature of the Renatus educational system.

Shannon:

You've done a lot of amazing things. You've built businesses, you've adapted, you're married, you have children, you have thousands of people that you mentor and that look up to you every day. What type of legacy to you want to make sure that you leave for them?

Bob:

Let me explain my motivation. The reason why I tick the way I tick, and believe me it's taken a lot of self-evaluation to figure it out, is that when I was a kid I had a father who was an alcoholic and a drug addict. His addictions created an enormous amount of financial stress in the home because we didn't know where our next meal was going to come from or what we would do when the power was turned off. I remember the bishop of our church was kind enough, when we lived behind him, to run an extension cord from his house over to our house so that we could run the refrigerator and watch Saturday morning cartoons after the power and the utilities had been turned off.

There was a lot of financial stress. I was a little kid and I didn't really understand it at that point, but as I started to grow it became more evident. The best thing that ever happened to Dad and the family was when he got caught for check fraud. That's what happens with addicts. They lie, they steal and they cheat, so that they can feed their addiction. Best thing that ever happened to him was he went away to jail for two years. Prison was a forced rehab for him.

When he was sober my Dad was a pretty brilliant guy. He graduated top of his class from University of Pennsylvania, and he went on to get his law degree from there. He was an assistant district attorney in San Francisco and had his own private practice up in Seattle. I mean, he was a smart guy. It was just addiction had taken a toll.

The other thing that meant a lot to me was my church, my faith. I served a two-year mission for my church. I loved every minute of it, being able to teach people how to apply gospel principles to bring them a lot of joy and happiness was rewarding. When you take that kind of philosophy and those correct principles and you put them into business with an investment like real estate, you can teach people a career path that will give them security, stability, financial freedom, and independence. You allow them to then give back to the community and to the world, and you can leave your kids and grandkids a lasting legacy from the inheritance they'll receive when you finally finish your time on this planet.

For me, all of that really has kind of led me to where I'm at today. My greatest satisfaction comes from seeing our students actually do what we teach them how to do and succeed. It comes from seeing them be good stewards of the money that they make. That's another thing, I'm not one of these flashy guys. I've got a nice house and I've got some nice cars, but I'm not driving around in a million-dollar Lamborghini.

There's not a lot of the flash and the bling and the nonsense with me because I don't want to set a bad example for my team. I would rather talk to them about cash flow. I would rather talk about assets. I would rather talk about balance sheets and profit and loss statements and how they can improve their lives and what they're doing to improve the lives of others. If I can make an impact on the community that really transforms their way of thinking so that they act and behave in that manner, we'll change the world.

What brings me the greatest amount of happiness is that I love seeing the positive changes in people's lives. In my first real estate company I dealt with a business partner who lost his focus. His ego got out of hand and he forgot about the people. It was all about his ego and his own self-aggrandizement. His world got so big that he just found himself working harder and harder to feed the monster of his creation. He had an enormous house and expensive cars and private servants and nannies and security details. He even had a jet.

I was just so disappointed with him; he set a bad example for the team. A lot of people in the community wanted to be like him. They started to make really bad financial decisions and leverage themselves into cars and houses and things that weren't producing income for them. He ended up filing for bankruptcy and had to liquidate millions in personal debt.

But life was always good for me because I've always lived well below my means. There's a massive lesson in that. Be a good steward of what you've got, live below your means, and you can still enjoy life, and I do. I enjoy life, and I don't have financial stress, and if everything but my real estate was taken away from me today I would still make a really nice income and never have to worry about money the rest of my life. I want people to have what I have. That's why I do what I do.

Jay & Nancy Abramovitz

Jay and Nancy Abramovitz have been successful business owners for over 30 years. Today, they reside in the Chicagoland area and together they run BTE Ventures, Inc., a company dedicated to building and inspiring a nationwide community of independent real estate investors and marketers, with the purpose of creating opportunities for financial stability and financial freedom for themselves and others.

After starting out in corporate America and honing their management skills for over a decade, they launched a sales and marketing firm in 1987. Since that time, they've represented dozens of manufacturers and importers in the home furnishings industry, including some of the very finest brands in the world.

In addition to formal degrees in Business Administration, Economics, and Psychology, Jay brings 35 years of real world experience in business development, management, and sales. As a business owner, Jay has always supported the underlying principles of building and sustaining teams to maximize the results of effort expended. He is recognized as a noteworthy communicator and a strong motivator. He has a keen ability to lead by finding creative solutions to problems.

Nancy holds degrees in both Art Education and Interior Design. She is a licensed interior designer, an artist, author, and a public speaker. Utilizing her design and project management skills in their real estate investing business has been a plus for making decisions on their fix and flip projects.

After training with the top-rated real estate investing program in the country, they became full time real estate investors and business development coaches. Jay and Nancy serve as part of the executive leadership for their local real estate investing community and are 5-Star Qualified Affiliates for the #1 real estate investment education program in the country. They are also proud supporters of the Responsibility Foundation and the Statue of Responsibility movement. They help to raise awareness of this important project and hope that everyone will understand its importance and become part of the movement. www.responsibilityfoundation.org/

Today Jay and Nancy spend their time building their personal portfolio of income producing properties while seeking ways to improve Chicagoland neighborhoods. They are changing lives by creating new awareness and new paths to action around the strategies of tax mitigation, interest reduction, and wealth creation.

With over a quarter century of experience marketing, selling, and managing front-end operations for small businesses, the transition to investing in real estate, marketing education products, and building sales teams has been a smooth one. Their attention is now focused on growing the pool of educated real estate investors and creating new income opportunities for independent minded entrepreneurs.

"At the core of our business philosophy, indeed the core of our living philosophy, is the ideal that integrity and honesty must be front and center in all aspects of our dealings with others. Business is nothing more than an act of commerce between people. Accordingly, the same ethical standards that apply to every-day life apply to all aspects of business conduct. We challenge ourselves every day and we invite others to do the same."

Shannon:

What inspired you to get into real estate investing?

Jay:

Well, I was inspired out of necessity. I had an interest in real estate investing for many years, but things always held me back. In fact, there were two things that were holding me back. First, I didn't have a support system that I could rely on to help me through the process. It's one thing to understand the concepts, but it's quite another thing to actually do it. Today, I work with a community of investors, and the overwhelming majority of them are not only willing but eager to help me and show me the way. They give me the benefit of their experience and to me, that is invaluable.

The other thing that held me back was motivation. Let me explain that. I've always been a highly-motivated individual, but when your career is going well and money is flowing into your life like it was in mine, there's a lack of, how shall I put it, pain. Well, fortunately or unfortunately, I went through a lot of financial pain, basically triggered by the financial collapse of 2008, and eventually it drove me to find another source of income. That led me back to real estate.

Now, I say back to real estate because decades prior I had invested in a few guru programs to learn about real estate investing. I got the concepts, but I never got into action because I didn't have that support system I just spoke of. In 2011, I experienced what I would have to call the perfect storm of having enough pain and finding the right support system, so I moved forward and got busy.

Shannon:

Awesome. Nancy, what about you?

Nancy:

I would like to just add to what Jay said, which is the story for both of us. Most of our working life has been spent in the home furnishings industry. Jay was an independent rep for high-end furniture manufacturers, and I ran an interior design business. We worked our own businesses, and we also helped each other. With the crash in 2008, those businesses began to wane, and we started looking for something else. The fields we were in were a close cousin to real estate. Although we weren't in real estate at the time, we were helping others to design and decorate their properties. We felt connected to the industry.

As we started looking for something else, we realized that we had to decide quickly because we were close to losing everything. We finally woke up to the fact that we were getting older and we needed to make a change in our financial path before it was too late. Forced to make that change, we came across this community of investors that have been a godsend to us. We learn with them, we work with them, and they help us move forward.

Shannon:
Awesome. Now, explain to me your relationship. Are you guys married, or are you business partners?

Jay:
We've been married 38 years, and yes, we're business partners as well.

Shannon:
Were you just drawn to each other because you had career paths that were somewhat connected, or did one of you change your trajectory when you met the other?

Jay:
When we met, our career paths were quite different. Career was not the glue that brought us together.

Nancy:
I was working for Tishman Realty, a commercial real estate company in Chicago. We met on a blind date, and then we married about eighteen months later. Through time, as we worked more together, I would say our interests began to meld. We both have interests in architecture, art, furnishings, and real estate. We saw that as we grew together, those interests just became stronger and they became our livelihood.

Shannon:

Tell me one of the best things about working together. Then, tell me one of the worst.

Nancy:

Okay, well one of the worst is that sometimes we step on each other's toes. We have different strengths, which is a good thing, but we don't always realize the other person may have already taken an approach toward tackling something that the other one is approaching in a different way. Sometimes we are rebalancing and coordinating our efforts so that we're trying to not do the same thing twice.

Shannon:

Okay.

Jay:

One of the things that I like about working with Nancy, and it should be obvious, is that our long-term objectives are identical. As a married couple, there's a strong commitment to each other. We're always working to each other's best benefit. It's not like we have to worry about divergent interests. That's definitely a strength that we have. Also, because we live together and we're together all the time, we're accessible to run our business. That's a negative and a positive, but it can certainly be a benefit. Sometimes it's hard to turn it off, but it's always accessible to us. Those are some of the best and some of the worst. We could probably have an hour-long discussion about that one question.

Shannon:

I bet we could.

Nancy:

I have another best to add and that's the trust factor. We trust that when one of us makes a decision, that we have the other's best interest in mind as well.

Shannon:

Right, which is huge, because so many people talk about how in real estate you need a strong team, and you guys are on the same team. It's amazing that you guys have this successful real estate investing career and have each other to lean on. Bravo.

Jay:

Hey, Shannon, you touched on the team aspect. Can I address that?

Shannon:

Yeah. That was going to be my next question. How important is it to have a strong team to back you other than just your spouse?

Jay:

Well, I think it's pretty important. I'd like to share our experience setting up our team as we got started. By the way, setting up and running a team is an ongoing process. I am of the belief that it will never be complete. It's always going to be tweaked and strengthened as we go. When we started, we were instructed and coached that you've got to have your team in place before you start. I confess that we didn't when we started. It was my opinion that the most important part of the team was the partnership itself.

I'm not just talking about Nancy and me but our other business partners. We started a partnership with our first partners, another husband and wife team, then we set up with our attorney. Those were our first and most important relationships. We decided to get started and we did just that. We went out and bought properties.

Then, we started to build the rest of our team as we moved forward. We connected with a realtor, then brought on the contractors. On the first jobs, we did some of the contracting ourselves, but we still needed some specialists. We just reached out to our community on an as needed basis. It was amazing. We had contractors available to us, sometimes within minutes of making a request. For example, if we were looking for a good tile setter we'd reach out to our network of investors. "Who do you know?" We'd get calls and texts back with referrals, then call those folks. We built our list and we built our team that way. It worked really well.

Shannon:

Now, is that advice you would give someone else, to just jump in and then build your team? Or do you think that might not be the best advice for some people?

Jay:

That might not be the best advice for some people but my real answer is, "It depends." Now, we happen to be connected to an extraordinary community and network of investors, so we had that available as a resource. In fact, I consider our community as one of our team members. That gives us access to everything we need. We knew we could tap that resource to no end, and we did. If you don't have a community like that, I would say you'd better get your team lined up before you start.

Shannon:

Nancy, do you agree with what he's saying? I know sometimes spouses really balance each other. Are you a "jump in, we have community." or are you a "jump in because I have faith in Jay"?

Nancy:

That's interesting. I would say I'm not necessarily a jump in person but that might describe Jay. He'll go with his gut. I am more of a planner in just about everything I do. I think about it, analyze it, and plan it. It takes me a bit longer to come to a decision on something. But the fact that we have the community and mentors around us boosts my confidence in coming to those decisions. I feel confident if Jay thinks it's okay, but I will sometimes go beyond that and ask if he's run the deal by someone else to see what they think.

For example, Bob Tierney, a senior member of our community, is one of our mentors and he's an excellent source for advice on pricing services and evaluating properties. I like to have other people's opinions. That's huge for me. We use our community to help us evaluate deals and decide how to best move forward on projects.

We always say that real estate investing is a team sport. When people try to go it alone, especially with no formal training, well, it can be a tough way to go. That's when people lose money, fail in their efforts, and quit. They grumble that real estate investing doesn't work. If you have the right education, apply it, and have the right mentors around you, it makes all the difference.

Shannon:
While we're talking about mentors, why don't you both tell me about a specific time when a mentor in your community helped you navigate past a potential pitfall?

Jay:
One comes to mind, but I have a problem. If I mention one name, I'll have to mention 100 names, and I can't mention them all. So, let me just say that I'm extremely grateful to everybody that has ever helped me on a real estate deal. There is a couple in our community that have become good friends of ours. He is an experienced carpenter. Recently, my partner and I were stuck on a project where we needed help installing a railing on a staircase. Now, my background is not in carpentry. My partner is much more talented than I am in that area but this particular project required a higher skill level.

I reached out to my carpenter friend, and I said, "We need some help on this. Can you come out and give us some guidance? Maybe just spend a half a day and show us what we need to do. If you help us with this, we'll buy you lunch." He did. He came out with another good friend and community member, and the two of them worked on the problem and got it resolved.

Now, the beautiful thing is that I would have been happy to pay them money, but they were happy just to take lunch. That's the kind of spirit that we have in our community. I could tell stories all day long about that kind of assistance.

There really is no end to this conversation. Those friends came to mind just now but there are dozens of other people who help us all the time. My biggest regret is that I can't name them all. Our community is a bottomless well, a limitless resource for us.

Shannon:

Amazing. I love paying people with lunch. Not only do you pay them with lunch, but then you get to spend that time together breaking bread.

Jay:

I've got to expand on that. Not only do we pay with lunch but also with gratitude. We reach out and actively seek help because it's such a great learning opportunity. Sometimes we learn and sometimes we teach. I can make my best strengths available to them any time they want. Sometimes it's talking to other investors and encouraging other people to join our community. They always know that they can tap into my strengths to bolster their weaknesses just as I tap into their strengths to bolster my weaknesses.

Shannon:

Perfect. Nancy, what do you have to add?

Nancy:

I want to add that we all come to the table with our own life experiences and our own strengths. Being new to this industry, we've had to rely on a lot of people to say, "Hey, what do you think? Is this going to work? How do you think I should go about this?" All kinds of questions. In most cases, we were very willing to learn and take the advice from more experienced people. On occasion, we haven't.

In one case, we were given advice on who not to work with. We didn't take that advice and we ended up having a huge problem. That was a big lesson learned. We've had to learn to listen to what more experienced people tell us. At a certain point in life you feel like you know everything you need to know. Getting into this line of work, we have realized how much we don't know and that we need to continue learning and pay attention to our mentors.

Shannon:

Your interior design experience can come into play on fix and flips, but I suppose it can also be dangerous. While you may be doing a great job of design, you may not be doing what the project requires.

Jay:

Shannon, it sounds like you've looked in on some of our projects because we have been guilty of over-designing and over-repairing a property or two just because of our background. It doesn't necessarily fit the project. You live and you learn.

Nancy:

And we have to trust our partners too. Because we come from high-end furnishings, we have to pay close attention to the numbers and not just go with what looks great. That's been a hard thing for me to swallow. We can't have our feelings hurt when we come up with a plan and our partners look at us like we're crazy. We have to be flexible.

Shannon:

All right, so tell me, what is your favorite strategy for acquiring a fix and flip?

Jay:

My favorite strategy is somebody in the community brings me a deal and says, "Hey, Jay, what do you think of this?" I'm only half joking because I don't really like going out and digging up the deals. Once again, community comes into play here. I don't like the research aspect of it, so I connect with people who specialize in that and bring us opportunities. My best resource for finding deals is our community.

Then, I go to work on taking whatever looks good and then getting creative putting the deal together. Do we want to negotiate seller financing? Is it right for a short sale? Or perhaps a subject to strategy? That's where my talent really shines through. I like to get creative and make something really interesting for the seller that benefits us as well. Everybody wins.

So, my best acquisition strategy is a network of people that bring me deals. There isn't a day that goes by that I don't have deals presented to me. All I have to do is answer my phone and open my email. By the way, that didn't develop overnight. That came about by developing relationships inside our community.

Shannon:
Perfect. In your financing part of the acquisition, you talked about subject to and you talked about short sales. Do you have a favorite financing option?

Jay:
Well, I've used private money, and I've used hard money. These days I try and avoid hard money. They call it hard for a reason. That's another lesson I learned. Today, I look for private money, especially on fix and flips. I like to bring private money into a deal in an equity position as opposed to a debt position. It costs me less up front, and it costs me less operationally to run the deal. I can do my deals under a lot less pressure than having to worry about interest accruing daily.

Today, we're working less on fix and flips and more on buy and hold properties, and we are actively seeking seller financing. Let me share a fix and flip deal that's in play right now. I don't even know if this will come to fruition, but we're negotiating on it.

There's a woman who has a property in the Chicago area. She's in her mid 70's. I don't know her. The deal came to me through a community member. He said, "Jay, this is the opportunity. There's an offer in front of this woman, with whom I have a personal relationship. The offer is for $125,000, and she's getting ready to make her last major financial transaction in life. She needs a retirement plan. The house needs about $50,000 in repairs, and it has an ARV of $275,000." All the numbers were lining up, but I don't like to put money in up front where I can avoid it.

I said, "Okay, let's do this. She has an offer in hand for $125,000. Let's offer her $132,500. We'll give her $7,500 more, but she will deed the property over to us now, with a lien against the property. We will pay the seller $132,500 on the back end, after it's rehabbed and when we close it to a retail buyer." We will bring the rehab money into the deal in an equity position. That's the proposal that's in place. If the woman accepts our offer, we will essentially acquire the property with truly zero money. Nothing out of pocket and no interest expense.

We now have a built-in expense of $7,500. That's the difference between the $125,000 and the $132,500. Essentially that's what it's going to cost us for money. It might take us six months to acquire, fix, and close out on the back end. That will be the bulk of our holding expense. I love that as a strategy because it takes pressure off me to raise the money to buy the property. I can now use my money sources on other deals. I love getting creative around building deals. That's what makes real estate so much fun to me.

Shannon:
Now, I understood everything you said, but role play with me on how you would communicate to this 75-year-old woman who's making a huge financial decision. She may not have real estate know-how. How are you going to get her to go with you versus the up-front cash that she can get with the other investor?

Jay:
Well, it always starts with having a conversation with, let's call her, Mrs. Jones. The first thing I need to understand is what Mrs. Jones' needs are. What are her immediate needs? What are her long-term needs? In this case, let's just assume that she doesn't have an immediate need for cash in hand, but she wants this cash to live out the rest of her life. I would say, "Mrs. Jones, you have an offer in hand for $125,000. We'd like to pay you more. Are you okay with that?" Of course, the answer would be, "Yes." "Here's the one caveat, Mrs. Jones. Instead of paying you $125,000 today, we'd like to pay you $132,500 in about six months."

"We'll pay you more in exchange for giving us more time to pay you. Your interest will be secured by the property itself. So you understand, we're going to fix the property up and then sell it to somebody else. A new family will come into the home that you've been living in for the past 50 years, and they're going to raise their family and they'll create a new generation of people enjoying life on this block that you've enjoyed over the years. That's our basic plan, if you can wait six months for the money—how does that sound to you?"

The conversation might go something like that. Mrs. Jones doesn't need to know all the details because it will only confuse her.

Shannon:

Right. I'll tell you what, you just sold me. I want to sell you my house in six months.

Jay:

Let's have lunch and we'll talk.

Listen, the key is this. When you're talking to home owners you always want to make the conversation about them because, frankly, it is about them. If you're not resolving their problem, then you're going at the deal the wrong way. If you can't solve their problem, then it's all about money, and it can't be all about money. Do I want to make money on the deal? Of course I do. I need to.

However, if I am solving the homeowner's problem, and I'm speaking to them and treating them with genuine care and respect, which I do, then we will connect on a human level and the seller will want to do business with me. I can do that and still make money. If I'm doing that then Mrs. Jones is going to want to do business with me more than she will want to do business with the investor offering her $125,000 cash now.

I'm having a conversation with her about the home that she loves, a house that can be a part of raising another family and keeping that neighborhood in tact as a solid neighborhood. That's what the home-owners want to hear. That's what they care about.

We just need to think as human beings and treat our sellers, business partners, and contractors that way. We need to treat them the way we want to be treated. The business goes amazingly well when you take on that attitude.

Shannon:

Perfect. Nancy, do you have anything you want to add to that?

Nancy:

Yeah. I tend to take on the role of devil's advocate because I'm the planner, the one that takes more time. Jay's the one that comes up with these great ideas. He's a great thinker when it comes to crafting deals and negotiations. He'll come up with an idea that he'll run by me. Then, I look at him and I think, okay, this woman might need money to buy her condo in Florida, or maybe to pay medical bills. She might need . . . whatever. That's what I think about. I'm the devil's advocate. Jay thinks of me as the one who looks for problems in the deal.

He says, "Don't look for problems." But I think it's important to do that so he can then go back to her with those possibilities in mind. He should be ready to speak to her on those subjects if necessary. Then, he can say, "Okay, I understand your situation, so how about if we do this?" He'll be ready for that conversation.

Jay:
I love that Nancy is always looking out for pitfalls and playing devil's advocate because in the example we just gave you, let's say that Mrs. Jones needs money to buy her condo in Florida, we'll just adjust the conversation. Instead of giving her $125,000 now or $132,500 in six months I'll ask, "What do you need to get situated in Florida? Do you need money to move? Do you need money as a down payment for your condo?" I'd rather buy that $132,500 property, which represents a $75,000+ profit to me, by giving her the $25,000 she needs to get situated in Florida. I can do that up front and pay her the balance on the back end. I'm completely flexible, so I love it when Nancy plays devil's advocate and finds the pitfalls.

We'll just address them.

Shannon:
Nancy, are you saying that if you're aware of the potential problems and you address them with Jay, it helps him because he can address them up front? Rather than having to say, "Let me get back to you on that." he can say, "Well, we thought of that and here's our solution." Is that an accurate assessment?

Nancy:
Yes, it is. It works well for us.

Shannon:
Perfect. So, what if she just said, "All I need is help packing."

Jay:

I'd say, "Done. Tell us when you want to pack and we'll have a crew there to pack."

Shannon:

I'd like to know, has that ever happened?

Jay:

I've never run into that scenario. However, let me share a story with you. This was a deal that we invested in but didn't get hands on. The lead on the deal negotiated with the seller who inherited the property. The seller was having trouble dealing with all the personal belongings remaining in the house. Our lead negotiator said, "You know what, if this is a big problem for you, why don't you just take whatever belongings you want, and whatever you don't want, just leave. We'll deal with it." The net result was this. The property was purchased with what turned out to be over $25,000 in estate sale profit just from selling off the furnishings, and we took a lot of stress off the seller.

Our job is finding solutions to problems. When we do that well, we do our business well.

Shannon:

Nancy, what is your favorite part about real estate investing?

Nancy:

I would say I have two favorite parts. One is the aesthetic part. I love looking at properties and architecture. I love envisioning what something can be. When I walk into a place and see it full of mold and in disrepair, I can envision it turning into some beautiful gem. That's just something I enjoy doing, and that's one of the parts that I love.

Another part of the business that I enjoy is the flexibility that it affords our family. It's not a 9-to-5 W-2 job. We don't have to answer to a boss. We make our own decisions.

Income in this business can ebb and flow, but if we manage it correctly, we can have a nice lifestyle. I enjoy the fact that we can take time off when we need it or want it. If we need to help a family member, or if we just want to go on vacation, we do it.

Shannon:
Jay, what about you?

Jay:
Well, I concur with Nancy on the flexible lifestyle. We enjoy that. We've been living that way for the past 35 years or so. Probably the most enjoyable part of the business for me though is structuring creative deals. I get turned on by finding creative ways to solve other people's problems. If we can help people out of a financial crisis or out of an emotional struggle around dealing with a real estate problem, that's a good day's work.

I love looking at a deal that someone's having a problem with. I treat it like a jigsaw puzzle. What's available to us? What are all the working parts? How can we make it fit in a truly creative way that nobody saw before? In the end, not only is everybody happy, they're thrilled. We come out on the back end with what we need and the seller gets what they need. That's what turns me on.

Shannon:
I love it. I have one more question. I'm going to have Nancy answer first. Think about your legacy and think about why you do what you do. Nancy, what is the legacy that you want to leave behind?

Nancy:
When I think about the mark that we'll leave on the world, I'm reminded of the physician's Hippocratic Oath. "First, I will either help the patient or I will do no harm." Next, they respect those people who have taught them and then they pass on that knowledge to those who follow. That's what I hope to do.

As leaders in our community, and as good citizens of the world, our aim is to lead by example. If we learn to do the right thing and put that knowledge to good use, then that knowledge must be shared with those who work with us now and with those who follow, whether they are members of our team or others out there in the world.

You know, our families still wonder when we'll get real jobs. The thing is, Jay and I don't have children, and we want a comfortable retirement for ourselves so that our nieces and nephews won't have to worry about having to take care of us. We want the burden of our existence to be on us, not them. And if we do need to lean on our nieces and nephews for assistance at the end of our lives, at least we want to be able to leave them something extra to help ease their burdens.

Shannon:
Thank you. Jay, same question.

Jay:
I'm so glad you asked that question. It brings to mind a conversation that I had with one of my favorite mentors in this business, a gentleman by the name of Bob Snyder. Bob once asked me what I wanted out of this business. I thought about it for a brief moment, and I said to Bob, "It's an interesting question because I'm at a point in my life you know . . . (I was approaching 60 at the time) . . . I've been in the place of earning lots of money and we've enjoyed a comfortable lifestyle. These days, although I need money to support the lifestyle I like, I'm thinking more about legacy." That's what I said. "It's time for legacy, Bob."

I want to make a mark on the world. When I'm gone, I would like to be thought of as someone who had a positive impact on other people's lives. I want to be thought of as someone who left the world at least a little bit better than he found it. While I certainly want to be comfortable in my life, this is not all about money. In the end, I want to be able to say that we helped people make their lives a little better, whether by way of creating, say, affordable housing to more people or by inspiring others to pursue their personal dreams and create their own unique personal legacies. I truly believe there is no greater good in the world than enabling other people to achieve more for themselves, their families, their communities, and even for the world at large.

In the end, I may not be able to see my impact on a worldwide scale, but I don't know; the final chapter of my story isn't written yet. I believe in the butterfly effect, which is to say that small actions in one place have the potential to start a series of reactions that can have truly profound impact in places that I may not even know exist. It's for that reason that I believe we really must be true to our core values and make sure that our actions reflect those values. We may be shaping the lives of people that aren't even born yet, people we will never even know.

Robert E. Asercion

Robert E. Asercion is a real estate investor and an assistant pastor in his local community. He is retired military and spent 26 years in the U. S. Navy. Robert is very much involved in his community; he is the Executive Director of Faith Food Fridays, a food outreach program for the community giving away free groceries and food to those in need. He is also the American Legion Commander for Post 603, Manuel L. Quezon veteran organization and a chapel-volunteer for David Grant Medical Center at Travis Air Force Base California. Robert received a BA in Business Administration from Columbia College, Missouri, and he is currently finishing his Master's Degree in Human Resource Management at Golden Gate University in San Francisco, California. He has been married to Giessell Asercion for 34 years and is the father to two sons, Christopher and Shawn, and one daughter, Rochelle. He has three grandchildren: one boy, Cyrus, and two girls, Zoe and Keira.

Shannon:
What inspired you to get into real estate investing?

Robert:
The leverage you have and the tax benefits that come along with it. You can buy an asset now and sooner or later it's going to appreciate. Not only that, if you're buying and holding a property, you can actually have passive income while deducting depreciation on that particular property for your taxes.

Shannon:
Have you always been a real estate investor?

Robert:
No, I actually just started a year and a half ago. I've always been curious about all those gurus you see on television. I've attended a couple of those in the past but never really understood anything until I really dug into a real estate education platform that I am now a student of.

Shannon:
What happened a year and a half ago that made you decide now is the time?

Robert:
We are an empty nest family right now. I am a blessed father with three children who are all married and a blessed grandfather with three beautiful grandchildren. I'm semi-retired. I retired from the military in 2003, after spending 26 years in the U.S. Navy. I am also a part-time pastor in a local church here in my community. A year and a half ago, I thought it would be a great time to understand and pursue real estate investing.

Shannon:
Thank you for your service, first off. I appreciate it.

Robert:

Thank you. It's was my honor and privilege to serve my country.

Shannon:

You're welcome. Once you got started in your education platform, what is one of the top real estate strategies that you have learned?

Robert:

Wholesaling. It doesn't really involve a lot of time and money. It's just making sure that you have the property under contract, whether it be a 'subject to' or an 'assigned to' contract with the owner of the property. A lot of times these properties are distressed and the owners need help. The investor then gives the homeowner options and places the property under contract. Once under contract, you can wholesale it to other investors or even the public who are looking for homes. You become the middleman between the seller and the other investor (buyer) and make a profit off the sale.

Shannon:

What is a 'subject to'?

Robert:

It's a piece of paper, a contract, that is exchanged between parties wherein a property is going to be subject to the agreement between the owner and also the buyer during contract negotiations on the property.

Shannon:

What was the other one you said, 'assigned to'?

Robert:

Yes, 'assigned to.' You can assign a contract to a person, or to an LLC, a company.

Shannon:

Explain to me an 'assigned to.' Explain to me why it's less risky than another option.

Robert:

Let's say I placed a distressed home under contract. I can have my name on the contract and have a few extra words added after my name, i.e., "and/or assigns." In doing so, I can assign the contract to another investor who has interest in the property. It's less risky because I have an exit strategy in which I can assign it to another individual or corporation. A lot of times we assign it to the investor's LLC and/or S corporation or C corporation. It's the smart thing to do because you don't want to bring the pain home if you get into a lawsuit or anything like that. The 'subject to' and 'assigned to' are contract vehicles, legally binding contract vehicles, that can transfer property ownership to the investor or the buyer. You don't have to go through the bank or anything like that as long as the owner agrees to the conditions that you're going to be helping the owner of the home in paying the mortgage. It could be a pre-foreclosure scenario. It could be a foreclosure scenario, or it could be just somebody that could no longer can make their mortgage payments because of a loss of a family member—the bread winner—and they're desperate. So you give them options to turn over their property via those two vehicles. The investor in return will make sure that the house doesn't go foreclosed on by making the debt service to the mortgage company. Bottom-line is, once under contract, the investor can re-assign it to another investor for purchase for a fee usually 10 percent of the ARV.

Shannon:

What is a short sale?

Robert:

A short sale is a condition where the owner has defaulted on their loan, and they're trying to sell it before it forecloses. The short sale can only take place when the note holder, usually the bank, is willing to short sale the property for less than what is owed on the debt or below the appraised value of the property. As a matter of fact, I have a short sale deal right now that is ready to close escrow in a few days. My LLC opened escrow on this property in August 2016, and we are now just getting ready to close escrow on the property. It can take a while to process short sale transactions. You have to be patient. Was it worth the wait? Absolutely! Knowing that you will have substantial equity in the property after closing escrow—I can fix & flip, buy and hold (rent it out) for passive income, and/or wholesale the property.

Shannon:
Why would you . . . Go ahead.

Robert:
Oh, why would you buy a short sale? Because a lot of times you are able to help the home owners protect their credit. The short sale, I believe, stays on your record for two to three years while a foreclosure stays on a person's credit file quite longer. I'm not sure about the number of years, but it's longer. It's almost like bankruptcy, seven years on your credit record. The other reason in buying a short sale is it gives you instant leverage already in the property because it has equity. So you help the homeowner, and if your calculations are right, make a profit in return as an investor.

Shannon:
Got it. What are some other creative ways that you can acquire a property?

Robert:
You can do tax liens and tax deeds. You can go on-line and go do to different states and participate in on-line tax deed and tax lien auctions, especially in Florida and Indianapolis. Many states hold an on-line and in-person tax deed and tax lien auctions. You got to know their bidding and their auction systems. You got to know how to get into county records. Need to do your "due-diligence." I have an on-line platform where I can go to different states and find out if there's a tax deed that's for sale. You can buy these for pennies to the dollar on-line. In a tax deed state, if it's not redeemed by the owner in the specified amount of time dictated by the city or county, and you're in first position, you can get ownership of the property just like that!

Shannon:

Explain what a tax lien is a little bit more to me. When you say you're in first position to buy the property, I'm not in real estate investing, so I don't know what that actually means.

Robert:

Okay let me first talk about tax lien certificates. In the U.S. there are tax lien states and tax deed states. In a tax lien state, homeowners that cannot pay their property taxes raise a red flag to the city because the property tax collected is used for revenue and salaries for their schools, police, and fire departments and for maintenance of the city or county. The property tax is revenue they need to run the city effectively. If not collected, the community is going to break down. To compensate for this, the city offers tax lien certificates to investors through an auction process. This allows the city to collect the money right away from the investor to take care of the city. Normally the interest rates on these certificates can go up to 30 percent depending on the city. If the homeowner redeems the tax lien, the investor gets paid on the amount of the tax lien and the corresponding interest rate. Could be quite lucrative. Not all states are tax-lien states. In tax deed states the homeowner can lose their property to the tax deed investor if not redeemed in time.

Shannon:

So simply because someone didn't pay their taxes they can lose their entire property?

Robert:

Yes, only if it's in a tax deed state.

Shannon:

I did not know that. That's super interesting. You also mentioned deeds. What is the difference between a tax lien or a deed?

Robert:

They're basically the same. Some states are called tax lien states.

Other states are called tax deed states. I believe California is a tax deed state. I got to make sure of that, but I'm pretty sure it's a tax deed state. The difference between a tax lien and a tax deed is that in a tax lien state scenario, if the homeowner pays the property taxes and interest it goes to the investor who bought the tax lien certificate with interest. Now, if the homeowner does not pay the property taxes in a tax lien state it cannot be sold nor refinanced until taxes are paid. In a tax deed state, however, if the homeowner does not pay the property taxes, the tax deed certificate holder can own the property because it is in a tax deed state, the investor is placed in first position on the deed. However, once redeemed by the owner, the money that they pay and everything with interest basically goes to you, the person that bought the tax deed.

Shannon:
The investor?

Robert:
Yes, the investor, so it's a win-win situation because the money was already used by the city because you already paid for it. And if the property owner pays the taxes that money paid to the city goes to the person who bought the tax lien/tax deed with the corresponding interest.

Shannon:
You said that in Florida and . . .

Robert:
Indianapolis.

Shannon:
… Indianapolis, but you currently live in the Bay area of California, correct?

Robert:
Yes. Yes.

Shannon:

Is it scary to you to know that you are investing in areas outside of your immediate control?

Robert:

It can be. You just have to get familiar with the process on how they do the tax- lien process per state. A lot of times there's "practice" online auctions so you can get familiar with their process. A lot of times you have to be there in person to participate. The ones that I did and tested were the online auctions in Florida and Indianapolis. Now for tax deeds, you have to really do your due diligence because you can end up owning the property.

Shannon:

If you're wanting to get started in real estate with little money or poor credit, are tax liens an option for you?

Robert:

Yes. it's not that expensive. You can buy them reasonably cheap and no credit check is required. Some of the money that's owed on the properties as far as property taxes are not that much.

Shannon:

What is another strategy if you're wanting to get started with little money or poor credit?

Robert:

Well right now I'm involved with my team with fix and flips, where we buy off market properties—properties that are being pre-foreclosed. This is a situation where the owner of the property receives a default letter from their note holder for non-payment of their mortgage. We approach the owner and we make an offer to purchase the property pending results of the property and pest inspections and title search. We ask them how much they owe on it and we make a reasonable offer to the homeowner. As long as there's a profit margin in there, and we compute the maximum allowable offer based on comparables in the area. There's a few formulas in real estate that you have to know and make your decisions off of that. I use an excel real estate spreadsheet to do my calculations. Make sure you double check your numbers. That's where the knowledge comes into play because real estate is a risky business. You've got to mitigate the risk with knowledge and also have a community where you can call fellow investors and get their advice.

Shannon:
When doing a fix and flip, what are some things that you should look out for?

Robert:
Well, you got to make sure that all the inspections are done, the current appraised value, and the comps. You don't want to fix and flip a house where the comparable is way different than the property that you're buying. You got to to do your due diligence and make sure. A lot of times the owner has disclosures, called the owner's disclosures so you the investor can find out what's wrong with the property. Ensure pest control and home inspection are done. Once you open escrow on it making sure that the title is clear and there are no liens on it.

Shannon:
What do you do if the title is not clear?

Robert:
If the title's not clear, let's say for example in the preliminary title report the property has a mechanic's lien on it. To clear the title, someone has to pay for it. This is negotiable between owner and buyer. Everything is negotiable between the owner and the investor (buyer). Now, if the homeowner cannot pay it off because maybe he/she lost a job or financially challenged, then the investor has to pay for that.

Shannon:
How can an individual benefit from a lease option?

Robert:

For a lease option, there are a lot of people that have good income, but a lot of them have challenged credit. Most of them can't qualify for a loan because of their challenged credit. What's nice about a lease option is if I, the investor, had a home I just purchased and rehabbed, I can offer that person that has challenged credit a lease option on the property. If the family or single person interested in the house has the capacity to place a down payment, i.e. $50,000, and is able to pay for the monthly mortgage, I would offer them a lease option. Within the three years the buyer exercises his right to purchase the property—lease option contract. If he defaults on the contract, I, the owner get to keep his $50,000. This example can look attractive to a lot of people that have good income but have challenged credit.

Shannon:
When doing a short sale, what should you anticipate?

Robert:

When doing a short sale, one should anticipate a long journey. As a matter of fact, I am ready to close escrow on one. I put it under contract August 2016, and we're just getting done with it now in July 2017. A lot of patience is needed because you're dealing with the banks, and the banks have their own process. It's a back and forth type of negotiation between the bank, the home owner, and the investor. Four parties need to agree: the investor, the home owner, HUD, and the bank. It's a pretty involved process.

Shannon:
Why does the homeowner need to agree?

Robert:

Well, the homeowner owns the property; they sign the contract that they're going to sell that house for a particular price. It has to be approved by the bank and the investors of the bank. HUD establishes certain guidelines in making sure that the price you're buying it for is not too high or too low for the bank. Most of the time the price is below market value.

Shannon:

So the one that you just closed on took 11 months. How long do they usually take from beginning to end?

Robert:

Well, it depends. Different banks have different processes. I've seen a short sale close in six months and another in three months. In this particular case, the one I'm in, it's taking a little longer, almost a year.

Shannon:

If someone wanted to invest in multi-family dwellings, what do they need to know?

Robert:

Oh, that's a different ball game. I know I've started my real estate class on that, but I haven't finished it yet. I have yet to dive into commercial real estate. With commercial property, and multi-families, they have cap rates where you can figure out your return on investment (ROI). It depends on the investor of course, but you have to have the knowledge in dealing with commercial real estate.

Shannon:

Can you learn everything you need to know from the library?

Robert:

Probably so; however, the real estate educational platform that I'm involved in covers a number of courses in real estate. It's not just only real estate. It's also financial literacy, getting out of debt, and how to manage your money. We have topics like velocity banking and sweeping strategies in paying off your home in five to seven years on a 30-year amortized loan. I believe a dedicated real estate educational platform is the way to learn real estate. Once learned, its applying what you learn on the deals that you make with the support of the community.

We have real estate communities all across the United States in different cities. It's just great to be part of it. We learn together and oftentimes invest together. It's just amazing to see how everybody helps out in the different deals that I've seen and been involved in.

Shannon:
How has real estate changed your life?

Robert:
Well, I have just been in real estate investing for a short period of time. But in that short period of time, I have learned a few strategies to leverage my income. With the short sale, I have right now, it gave me leverage because the house was below market value. When we close escrow there should be equity in the property. It was my friend and investor partner that told me about the property. He put a bug in my ear saying, "Hey, partner, this house is going to be for sale but it's still off market." After that, I got excited and contacted the listing agent. We put a bid on it and the homeowner and bank accepted our offer, so that started the journey. I now have leverage because the property was bought below market price, and it's worth a lot more today than when we first put a bid on it.

Shannon:
In your business, how do you help other people learn more about real estate investing?

Robert:
By marketing the on-line educational platform I purchased to family, friends, and acquaintances. We also have regular real estate opportunity meetings on Thursday evenings in our North Bay office. We are getting ready to close escrow on a fix and flip deal in Vallejo, California. Once it's closed we will start rehabbing the place. We currently have two properties under contract that are ready to be rehabbed. Once we start, we normally set-up "Real Deal Tours" for our students and future students who have not signed up yet for their educational platform. During the tour, the investors of those

properties get to show and tell how they got the property, how much was the property, rehab costs, future selling price, and how much they will make after flipping the property.

Shannon:

What is the number one mistake that you think people make from acquisition to buying their first investment property?

Robert:

Going in there with no knowledge of real estate and how to structure the deal using entities to protect their assets. They might have the money and capital but not the knowhow and protection they need. Some buy properties under their name and social security number. That could be a recipe for disaster.

Shannon:

You just said they use their own name and their own social security number to buy a home. Who's name?

Robert:

Their own personal name. Nothing wrong with that, but if you're an investor and you plan on buying multiple homes later on, you want to mitigate the risk of being in the lawsuit, especially from tenants or from the community. The best way to do that is to have an entity like a Limited Liability Company (LLC), S-Corporation, C-Corporation, or a holding company that you can put your real estate in. You don't have to use your social security number if you use an entity because each entity has an EIN number.

Shannon:

What is cash flow, and why should it be such an important focus of your business?

Robert:

Cash flow is very important because in real estate, you have to fund your deals with cash. If you have a lot of rentals, it's a win-win situation.

Why? Because the person renting your home is paying for your real estate mortgage. You might have a little negative cash flow in there, or maybe positive cash flow. Nine out of ten times, the investor will have a positive cash flow in that particular rental. That gives you an advantage in raising capital because you have cash flow coming in every month.

Shannon:
What does HELOC stand for?

Robert:
Home Equity Line of Credit. It's a loan from the bank where the collateral is the equity of the property. You have to qualify for it. You have to have good credit. You have to have equity in the house

Shannon:
How does learning multiple investing strategies protect and accelerate investing success?

Robert:
It comes to a point where a seasoned investor looks at a certain property and knows in their mind what they're going to do with that property. I know every investor has their own plan and way of doing things. But deep inside they know how many rentals they want to have, how many fix and flips they want to do. Having the educational platform is key in making and backing your decisions. Knowledge of real estate is paramount.

Shannon:
How has your education in real estate changed the way that you invest?

Robert:
I gives me a lot of confidence to do deals knowing that I have the knowhow.

Shannon:
When you began your real estate investing career, how important was it for you to find a team to surround yourself with?

Robert:

Very important. I believe in teams. Being in the military, we worked as a team. In real estate investing, I work with my team who are also students of our on-line educational platform. There's actually four of us as investors in our team. We also have our realtor, our contractor, and our lawyer who is also part of the team. We try to make sure that everything is equally divided amongst us as far as what needs to be done in a real estate project.

Shannon:

Are you in North Bay, Napa, area?

Robert:

Actually, our office is located in Walnut Creek, California, but our main office is in Sacramento. We're expanding. We're slowly expanding.

Shannon:

Your mentor, your main mentor, is in Sacramento?

Robert:

Yes, my main mentor is in Sacramento. There's actually a marketing side to what we do, and a real estate side. And we want to balance that. The marketing side is the on-line educational platform. You can share with others—you get compensated for that if someone registers and becomes a student. At the same time, we're also doing real estate. It's simple: take the classes that are available in our educational platform and apply what we learn by doing the real estate deals.

Shannon:

How has a mentor or mentors in your real estate investing helped you to navigate potential pitfalls?

Robert:

Well, the practitioners that we have teaching the classes in our educational platform are all seven-figure earners. They're an expert in their field, and a lot of them are authors of various real estate books. That says a lot, being an expert in their particular field. Most of them have been in the real estate industry for 25, 30, 40 years. They travel all over the United States visiting our satellite offices in various cities mentoring students. When they come to Sacramento, we get to meet our practitioner in person, and ask questions.

Shannon:

What advice would you give to someone who is allowing fear to hold them back from starting in their career?

Robert:

Yeah, there's a lot of people that have a lot of gifts and talents out there, but there's also a lot of people that don't have the right mindset. Robert Kiyosaki talks about that in his book Rich Dad, Poor Dad. He talks about having the right mindset and fear is one of those factors that hinders a lot of people from doing what they possibly could do and become successful. Fear is holding them back. That's one of the biggest challenges that we have as mentors to people coming in and becoming a real estate student. They have the talent, they have the capability to become a real estate investor; however, their mindset is focused on fear.

Shannon:

Why do people succeed at real estate?

Robert:

Well, first and foremost a lot of people succeed in real estate because they have the real estate education. Real estate is a risky business and must be mitigated by knowledge. Secondly, shelter is one of the necessities in life to survive. We need to survive, right? I was listening to the radio about a week ago. They were talking about the San Francisco Bay Area housing crisis. According to the report, the Bay Area needs 70,000 more housing units to keep up with the influx of people coming in. Even though the market is a little slow as far as building homes, you can see that in real estate there's always going to be a need to build homes and have homes. I think that's one of the biggest reasons why people succeed in real estate.

Shannon:

Do you think that real estate investing success is dependent on a strong economy?

Robert:

Not really, because when the housing economy collapsed in 2008, all the veteran investors lost a lot of their assets. But then again, there was a lot of investors who started buying these assets at the same time for cheaper prices.

Shannon:

How does real estate allow you to earn massive and passive income?

Robert:

You earn massive income because you can have multiple assets you can rent out. All of these assets appreciate through time. Leverage is important because you're having your money work for you. Whenever you have money working for you that's multiplying your efforts

Shannon:

Most millionaires and billionaires have investments in commercial real estate. Why do you think that's so?

Robert:

According to Forbes magazine, real estate is still ranked number three in the investment portfolios of America's millionaires and billionaires. Commercial real estate is very appealing to high end investors because of the great return on their investment. That's where the big boys play.

Shannon:

Do you see yourself eventually expanding into commercial real estate?

Robert:

Why not? If the opportunity comes, sure.

Shannon:

The last question is what type of legacy do you want to leave?

Robert:

I want to leave a legacy for my family, but it doesn't extend only to my family. I want to help people, the less fortunate people. As a pastor, I used to go on medical mission trips to the Philippines every year—it's part of our mission's ministry in our church. There's a lot of work that needs to be done there. If I was to leave a legacy, and the Lord blesses me, I would like to make a difference in the lives of the unfortunate and poor in the Philippines by helping them spiritually, physically, and monetarily.

Benjamin Octavio Gallego III

When I graduated from college with an associate degree, I immediately began working for the Philippine Long Distance Telephone Company. I aspired more for my life; and this, coupled with a desire to see the world, led me to go work in Paris. I had a dream job in France, and I travelled all over Europe having fun while earning money. I married to my long-time girlfriend Maria Justina Tisado, a nurse practitioner. We emmigrated to the States and settled in Vallejo, California. We are blessed with three children, the eldest a boy now studying at San Jose State University. Also two girls, one is in high school and the other in middle school. I am presently working at Napa State Hospital as an electrician. My cherished dream is to retire early and enjoy life with my family. So, I got interested with real estate investing to make my dream come true sooner.

Contact info
Gallegorealestate@gmail.com
www.gallegorealestate.com

Shannon:

What inspired you to get into real estate investing?

Ben:

My knowledge about real estate was inadequate; however, I am a doer and have a positive attitude. I knew friends in real estate who made good by financially working in their own time rather than those having 9–5 jobs. So this inspired me to get into real estate, and acquiring more knowledge and being actively involved in the business is the only way to go.

Shannon:

So if someone were to want to get into real estate and they had very little money or poor credit, what advice would you give them about how to get started?

Ben:

Personally, I believe that very little money or poor credit is not a hindrance in going into the real estate business. I have heard countless stories of very successful real estate entrepreneurs who started their businesses from practically nothing and were armed only with the willingness to learn and the strong determination to succeed.

Shannon:

How has your education in real estate investing changed the way that you invest?

Ben:

Thanks to my recent education in real estate investing, I now fully understand the concept of step by step, one process at a time in doing my business. Real estate investing is a tough job; but now, by being more knowledgeable with all the facets of the business, I can avail different kinds of strategies and make early projections of the probable outcome for each strategy being employed.

Education is the key to understanding real estate investing. It lessens the risks in doing business. The wealth of knowledge an individual gains from education will surely improve the mindset and how to think and speak, as well as hot to present oneself in different business interactions.

Shannon:
What is one of the top real estate strategies that you have learned?

Ben:
The top real estate strategy that I've learned, I would say, is in short-selling. Previously, I got most of my information from the internet. With my recent education in real estate investing, I realized that my knowledge was inadequate, and now I am better prepared and more realistic in my approach in doing my business.

Shannon:
What is a short sale?

Ben:
When you sell a property that is less than what you paid for it is a short sale.

Shannon:
How long does the short sale process usually take?

Ben:
Based on my actual experiences and with my limited knowledge then, in short sales, it takes from six months or more depending on many factors that may affect the property. Here in California, the short sale process is so frustrating and time consuming.

In the recent real estate crash, we lost our own home. We tried to keep our property which we learned to love and value for about three years, paying off our lenders while trying to negotiate for better terms. Realizing that all of our efforts proved futile, my family decided to short sell it. Many of my neighbors already left, though some tried to hold on to their property for as long as they could. The lessons I learned from my sad experience made me decide to know more about short-selling so that I may be able to make it work for me in the future and just maybe also help my neighbors.

Real estate investing is a very interesting field. Short selling is only one aspect and I incorporate it to the whole real estate business as it is very relevant right now.

Shannon:

What strategy can you combine with a short sale?

Ben:

As in any business transaction, you may need several strategies to succeed. There is the financial side, the upgrading of the property if needed, and also the projected over-all cost and profit. In a short sale, you buy or take over a property usually at a low price.

Shannon:

How about public auction or a 'subject to' the terms of the mortgage?

Ben:

I am more interested in properties 'subject to' the terms of the mortgage as I can help people make the most of their properties in short sales. By using all the knowledge gained from experience and education, when the transaction is completed there is always that uplifting feeling that I feel aside from the monetary gain.

Shannon:

All right, so what is the number one mistake an individual makes when buying their first investment property?

Ben:

Lesson number one that I learned is people buying their first investment property usually lack sufficient knowledge of the real estate business. Most people, and that included me, rely on what others say. These things usually end up in mistakes, and mistakes can be very costly. So, to minimize the risk, talk to trusted professional in the business, or, better yet, get a good education in real estate investing.

Shannon:

How has real estate changed your life thus far?

Ben:

Being involved in real estate changed my life for the better. I took this education principally for my personal development. And I like the outcome of my education for this is really what I have been dreaming of, to be my own boss.

Shannon:

And what is that? What do you like the most?

Ben:

I want to be a bank or a lender someday.

Shannon:

You want to be a bank—

Ben:

Yeah, I want to be the bank or lender engage in real estate. However, in order to be a lender, one must have the means and knowhow in the areas of lending.

Shannon:

So is real estate investing success dependent on a strong economy?

Ben:

The answer is both a yes and a no.

Shannon:

Why yes?

Ben:

Yes because if the economy is strong, more people can afford to buy a home. Real estate is the primary beneficiary of a vibrant economy.

Shannon:

That's okay. Why no?

Ben:

No because shelter is one of the basic needs of man. Even in the worst of times, people will buy homes, maybe not in the same scale as in times of prosperity.

Shannon:

What's an example of a way that you can help someone in a weak economy?

Ben:

A weak economy affects different people in different ways also. In a weak economy home prices are mostly down. This can be the most appropriate time for people with a low budget to buy a home. Their main concern is how to finance their purchase. That is where I can be helpful with my education and experience in looking for strategies best suited for them. For people who want to dispose of their properties because of financial hardship, I can also help the find ways that will be most advantageous to them.

Shannon:

On that note, what is cash flow, and why is it important?

Ben:

Cash flow is the cash on hand and also the liquid assets that are easily convertible to cash. Cash flow is very important for it is a gauge of the viability of the business.

Shannon:

So what is cash flow?

Ben:

Cash flow is the difference between the incoming cash from all sources and the outgoing cash or expenses. With adequate cash flow, the business can operate smoothly; however, with very little cash flow there would be a need for outside financing so as not to hinder the business operation.

Shannon:

How does real estate allow you to earn passive and massive income?

Ben:

Real estate can mean passive income because of the growth in the equity of the property which can easily be converted into cash. A good idea in real estate attracts many investors making available many business opportunities for massive income.

Shannon:

What's the difference between massive income and passive income?

Ben:

A passive income is an income that is earned with little or no effort, like dividends and royalties. Massive income is that which comes from multiple sources. The best strategy in business is how to convert a passive income into a massive passive income.

Shannon:

How does learning multiple investing strategies protect and accelerate investing success?

Ben:

Learning and understanding the different kinds of strategies in business through education, and applying it, will mean more opportunities for success. Not only the success of having money but also success in life. Education eliminates guess-work in business. Hard earned money and the trust of many people in your business makes it imperative to make sure that your investment is sound.

Shannon:

How have mentors in your real estate investing helped you to navigate potential pitfalls?

Ben:

My mentors have been good to me. They have been helpful in better understanding proper business practices. They are always there for me ready with the right information and guidance in all undertakings.

Shannon:

Do you have a specific story that you could share about a mentor in your life and how they have helped you?

Ben:

I consider my mother way back in the Philippines in my younger years as my first and foremost mentor. She made me aware of the value of hard work, savings, and education. But most of all, honesty in all my endeavors. She gave me my first job at seven years old as an errand boy in our family, while never neglecting my schooling.

Shannon:

Do you have someone specifically that you admire more than others? Or a favorite mentor?

Ben:

I am fortunate that all of my mentors were good. When my father passed away when I was seven years old, I tended to look at all my elders as my mentors. I admire those that succeed professionally and those who became wealthy. However, I tried to emulate most those that have very good families.

Shannon:

All right. Tell me, have you done, or what do you know, about whole selling, and how can whole selling create wealth?

Ben:

I just did one whole sale just a few months ago here in my area. I partnered up with somebody in my group to undertake our business. I called a realtor to help us, then make an offer. After closing the deal, we made a few thousand.

Shannon:

So explain to me when you say that you found the whole sale deal and you called the realtor; here did find that deal?

Ben:

I found that deal in my area just a couple of blocks from our place. I saw the signage that a property was for sale, and then I called the realtor for more information. After analyzing the whole deal, we made an offer. We won the highest bid and we acquire the property. After a few days, we wholesale it to another person; and that's how we did the whole selling through our cooperative efforts.

Shannon:

What advice would you give to someone who is allowing fear to hold them back from beginning their real estate investing career?

Ben:

I would advise them that fear in starting their real estate investing career is normal just like in any other business. Fear makes us very careful, makes us think and work harder. On overcoming fear, I always keep in mind that there are always ways of doing the right way to be successful, and one of them is education. I always think about my dreams are bigger than my fear.

Shannon:

My next question is, were you afraid to get started, and what did you do to overcome the fear?

Ben:

Of course, fear was very much present. At my age, with responsibilities to my family, I hesitated to take my chance. However, my big dreams were so overwhelming that I had to test my limits if I wanted to succeed in life. So I prepared myself primarily by education. With education and doing it the right way, one can never go wrong.

Shannon:

So what do you think makes people successful in real estate investing?

Ben:

As for me, to be successful in real estate investing means lots of hard work, determination, right education, and focus in your work and commitment.

Shannon:

When you began your real estate investing career, how important did you feel it was to establish a team to help you be successful?

Ben:

The cooperative efforts of a team in business not only lessen the risk for the individual members but also means better planning and shared efforts in undertaking the business at hand. Being new in the real estate business, I value all the help I can get from all the members of the team. Working for a common goal gives the business more than an even chance to succeed.

Shannon:

In your business, how do you help others learn more about real estate?

Ben:

For me, anything that I do is more rewarding if I am able to share my knowledge with others. Presently, in our group or team, we are doing some real estate offers. In our meetings, we exchange ideas and continually learn from one another. Our team mission is not only to help ourselves but to help others in our business.

Shannon:

What kind of legacy to you want to leave?

Ben:

I want to give my family a legacy that they can be proud of. I want them to remember me for being honest, helpful, and a good family provider. I also want to be remembered as a doer, never handicapped by poverty, inadequacy of education, or few opportunities in life.

Robin Haley

Robin Haley has spent most of her life in the Pacific Northwest. She grew up in a very small town in Northern Idaho. It is that simple beginnings that bring out the best in all that she does. After attending college at Washington State University, her attempt to change the world started in health care. While spending most of her time helping others to understand Medicare and debuting a generic drug roll out program to rural communities, she dreamed of something bigger. Venturing out on her own resulted in the awakening of her creative spirit.

Robin has experience in creating and building businesses and devising simple and effective methods to generate income. Part of her success is practicing candor when it comes to giving people "real world" information. Truth, respect, and complete disclosure are the corner-stones of her relationship-building philosophy. Volunteering is also a prominent element in Robin's life. She is heavily involved in The Elks Lodge and, among other involvement, started a Girl Scout troop that has exploded into a troop of 38 young ladies. Through the Elks organization, Robin also chairs a Children's Therapy Program operated solely on donations. Recently, Robin was awarded The Elks, Northern District, Polly Garland award for servant leadership and community.

When she is not passionately investing in her business or volunteering, she divides her time between being on the family boat "Conundrum" in Puget Sound or pheasant hunting in South Dakota with her partner of 12 years and their two Vizslas.

Shannon:
What inspired you to get into real estate?

Robin:
You know, that's a great question. I didn't think I was interested in real estate until I had spent over 20 years in healthcare and ran my I.T. Company for 10 years. Once I closed Holistix Solutions, I knew two things. I didn't want to go back to a J.O.B., and I didn't have the funds to start up a new business venture.

Shannon:
Did you meet someone during your research, or did you just decide wow, this is it?

Robin:
When I started to look into real estate as a career, it was actually at the suggestion of a friend. I spent time shadowing a talented and experienced realtor during the time I was researching real estate. I found a great online real estate school that prepared me for my real estate license exam, and I was gearing up to take the test when I learned about real estate investing. Once I started researching more, I knew this was it! — for a variety of reasons. But most importantly, I wanted to do something for me. Real estate has really allowed that opportunity for me to see what I could do on building my own dream.

Shannon:
According to Forbes magazine, real estate is one of the top three ways that people become wealthy. Why do you think that is?

Robin:

Having real estate is a key ingredient in our daily lives. You need shelter. The income opportunities in real estate can be difficult, but rewarding, if you know what you're doing and have a strategy on what you are looking for.

Shannon:

If someone was going to get started in real estate, what would you recommend they do first?

Robin:

The first thing I would recommend to anyone is find a group, find an education, find a mentor, find a way of just immersing yourself in the world of real estate so that your decision to become a real estate investor is an informed decision. HGTV makes it look easy. It isn't!

Shannon:

How have mentors in your life helped you to navigate potential pitfalls?

Robin:

That's a great question. Having the perfect mentor for a specific situation is pivotal. I have a variety of mentors that have provided guidance in an array of situations since my childhood. Mentors are so valuable and important as you go through the different stages of things in your life. With this latest opportunity of moving forward with real estate, I have such a great group of mentors in my wheelhouse. My real estate investor community is amazing. The value that each brings to the table is sometimes overwhelming. In real estate, a property can become so personal and take on a life, like a needy pet. It is nice to have the mentor community I do, to talk me off the ledge when I can't see a bigger picture.

Shannon:

What is the number one mistake an individual makes when buying their first investment property?

Robin:

Well, that goes back to making it personal; and while that can get in the way, analysis paralysis is probably my number one. I spend too much time thinking about it and not doing it. I am getting much better though.

Shannon:

What advice would you give to someone who is allowing fear to hold them back from starting their real estate investing?

Robin:

It's such a great question because there isn't any one-real specific answer to that. When I purchased my very first piece of property in Spokane, Washington, I didn't have any idea what I was doing and was terrified. While the process was extremely overwhelming, I did it! I don't know if the "fear" goes away. I still get nervous and I don't see it necessarily as a bad thing either. When you are experiencing fear you certainly know you're alive and that you're challenging yourself. Doing something that's outside of your normal freaks people out.

Shannon:

If you're starting with a little bit of money or poor credit, what are some strategies to get into real estate?

Robin:

If you are wanting to get your feet wet in real estate, wholesale is a great place to start. It takes little money and no credit. What it does take is your time. You need to find the properties, do your due diligence on the numbers, and get it under contract. Wholesaling is a great way to get started.

Shannon:

What are some creative ways that people can find properties to wholesale?

Robin:

There are a lot of creative ways. Driving around is probably my favorite. I take my two dogs on walks to different areas in and around Puget

Sound. I enjoy checking out the neighborhoods. I LOVE finding "the house" in distress. It means that I can potentially help the person who owns it. Another creative way is an estate sale. It's a great way to find out a lot about the house. The others that aren't so creative are your obvious choices, the court house or other public records, like legal notices in a local paper.

Shannon:
What do public records have to do with wholesaling?

Robin:
Well, they share with you if a home is in foreclosure or probate. You can also review wills or other legal documents to determine heirs, who are now the property owners or if there was a divorce. There is a TON of information that can help you do your detective work in finding a property owner that could use your service.

Shannon:
When doing a short sale, what should you anticipate?

Robin:
Buying a short sale is a great possibility for those with knowledge and patience to get the deal done. Knowing your risks beforehand can help avoid a lot of pain and frustrations.

Shannon:
When doing a fix and flip, what do you want to look out for?

Robin:
Wow! So many things. My top would be making sure you have the right team. People think that they can flip houses easily. Unfortunately, most are disappointed with the initial results. A successful flip is one that you make money on. It isn't about quadrupling your money. Next would be structural issues. You really want to avoid cracked foundation walls. That can eat into a profit margin.

Shannon:
How does real estate allow you to earn massive and passive income?

Robin:
Having real estate in your retirement portfolio is just smart. Who wouldn't think it was great when you have an investment, a limited partnership, or another enterprise that is sending you "Mail Box Money" for the duration of time that you have the asset? The passive income or cash flow can be massive over time as you build your real estate portfolio.

Shannon:
How has your education changed the way that you invest?

Robin:
It has changed completely. Understanding the benefits of building business credit is going to generate hundreds of financial options for me in future real estate deals. The velocity banking alone will allow me to quickly pay down mortgages and other loans in as little as seven years or potentially less. I wish I had the knowledge that I have now when I bought my first house in Spokane. Having a strong foundation is the best base to any strategy, real estate or otherwise. Education is what gave me the knowledge and added value that I am able to bring to the table with other real estate investors. While I continue to get my "feet wet," I haven't settled on a personal "like" in real estate yet. I do believe Buy and Hold will be my main focus though; the potential passive income is great for a retirement package.

Shannon:
What is one of the top real estate strategies you have learned?

Robin:
Don't analyze it to death! Sometimes you just have to trust in yourself enough to just do it!

Shannon:

When building your business, how important was it for you to build a strong team?

Robin:

Having a community of likeminded individuals around you that bring a specific value, have strong virtues and integrity, and are accountable for their actions is a perfect recipe for success. I am currently working with several of my team mates on multi-family or other commercial real estate for one of my investors and on another team that we have been busy raising $2millon in private money. Having strong individuals around you that build a team is, like I said, "the perfect recipe"!

Shannon:

Do you feel like one or more positions on the team are more important than others, or do you feel like you're all equally important?

Robin:

Oh, I would say we're all equally important. Everyone brings a certain value. There's things I don't know. There's just certain things that I won't know, and that's where I count on others who have a strength in an area that's a weakness of mine, so each one of us bring a different value, which makes us all very equal.

Shannon:

Do you feel that real estate investing success is dependent on a strong economy?

Robin:

No. Not at all. I believe that with the education I have and the knowledge that I am gaining on real estate that any economy, weak or strong, will allow for success.

Shannon:

How do you think you can have success in a weak economy?

Robin:

Fortunately even in a weak economy, people still need a place to reside and business owners still need a place to conduct business. Whether its storage facilities, grazing farm land, or RV parks, you need a place to do it! Why not own it?

Shannon:

What is one of the investment strategies that you can use in a weak economy?

Robin:

Strategy in weak economy, of course, is buy, right? Money is harder to get in a weak economy so having cash available is key.

Shannon:

What is cash flow, and why should it be such an important focus of your business?

Robin:

Having access to additional monthly income allows you to invest in your business and build on to your real estate portfolio. Lack of cash or inadequate cash reserves or access to cash are some of the biggest reasons small businesses fail.

Shannon:

What is it? What is cash flow exactly?

Robin:

I think of cash flow as, well, picture a business checking account. If more money is coming in than is going out, you are in a "positive cash flow" situation. Cash flow is a revenue stream that has been developed by something you're doing or something you've acquired. Cash flow could be something as simple as owning a rental home or several rental homes or a commercial building or public storage. Cash flow is money that's being generated outside of what you currently doing. Cash flow allows you to invest back into your business.

Shannon:

If someone wanted to invest in multi-family dwellings, what do they need to know?

Robin:

I am very excited about multi-family. It was recently added to our education curriculum, and I am learning a lot as I dive in! A couple of things that I have found in multi-family is that you have two categories: small or large. Value of a small multi-family is determined by what similar houses down the street are selling for. Value on a large multi-family is mainly determined by comparing the ROI one would achieve with that of other commercial properties down the street. So basically, it is based on the ROI an investor would achieve if they did not use a loan. I am still in the learning phase with multi-family and am excited to do my first one.

Shannon:

What do you feel like you need to learn before you can invest in multi-family dwellings?

Robin:

There is a lot to learn for sure. I think that understanding income valuation and cap rate is probably the main thing. On multi-family, and I am talking about or five or more doors, it really ceases to be a "hobby." You really have to make it more of a business or its own entity with its own insurance, etc. This is where you really have to trust the numbers and separate emotion from the transaction.

Shannon:

All right. How can a real estate investor benefit from tax liens?

Robin:

Tax liens are a unique opportunity that can provide a knowledgeable investor with excellent rates of return, in some cases, but can also carry a lot of risk. You really need to understand the pitfalls that come inside that market. Once you have decided what type of property you want and, again going back to due diligence, in some cases the current value of the property can be less than the lien. Dividing the face amount of the delinquent tax lien by the market value will give you an idea of what your return or ratio would be. A rule is that if it is over 4 percent ratio, you probably want to stay away from it. Unfortunately, my first tax lien was not a great experience and a complete nightmare. I'm kind of reliving the nightmare of the tax liens that I got into right now, and knowing what I know now I would have never done it.

Shannon:
Share the story of the nightmare, of the tax lien you got into, and then tell me what you could have changed so that you could have been more profitable from it.

Robin:
This took place quite some time ago, well before I got into real estate education. My partner and I went in with another couple actually who we believed to have a lot of knowledge around investing. Unfortunately, we didn't have a contract with our new-found business partners either. (Two lessons learned: never go into business with ANYONE without some contractual obligations.) Anyway, back to the nightmare. Neither I nor my partner checked out the property. We assumed it had potential. Since there really is no room for "creative financing," I pulled money out of my savings and we went to auction. I am using the term "we" loosely. WE actually didn't go, so what we purchased was sight unseen. The Readers Digest version is that after a long battle we ended up quit claim deeding the property back to the original owners, and I lost all that I had put into it. It didn't have a clear title. We couldn't just "rehab" it. Apparently, it was a drug house back in the day and it required basically being torn down. We didn't have the $30k+ to meet the county requirements, and while it was a sad, friendship ending learning experience, I am glad that it happened. It was one hell of a teachable moment.

Shannon:
How can you find out if it's in a tax lien because it was a drug house?

Robin:

You know, I am not sure. I haven't been interested in tax liens, so I am not sure. I would think it would be available through legal records.

Shannon:

In your business, how do you help other people learn about real estate?

Robin:

By doing. I have shared many stories on how my team members helped me with real estate, and it was always by doing. I was stuck in an analysis paralysis, you know? It was fear, you bet, but it was more of 'I'm going to analyze this to the nth degree to make sure that it's a good deal.' Unfortunately, by the time I did all my analyzing, the deal was no longer available. You just have to 'Do It.'

Shannon:

How do you want people to remember you?

Robin:

My family is very important to me. I am always ready to help regardless of the situation. I think my little sister would say I would be remembered as being gregarious, kind, trustworthy and sometimes obnoxious, but I always have a smile on my face. For me, I grew up just a very simple farm girl in northern Idaho. We were all about church and family. That was it. I didn't realize growing up that we were poor. I really didn't. I mean, I never wanted for anything. I really felt like I had everything. It was after I had left home that I understood how financially poor we were. Money has never been a big piece in our family. It simply is not what we are about. I don't want to make it sound as though money is evil—it isn't! It just isn't what I am about. For me it really is about love, family, and faith. Those are the three big things to me in my life: love, family, and faith. I think that sums it up.

John Harmon

John Harmon was born on a Dairy farm to hard working Midwestern parents. He learned the value of education and the joy of helping others from his mother who was a Registered Nurse for over 40 years.

His Dad never graduated the sixth grade and lived his entire life as an extremely hard working blue collar worker. John learned how to be proficient working with his hands and the desire to reach for the stars from his father

After high school, John Joined the US Navy and entered into the Nuclear Power program. While in the military, he attained highly advanced formal training and certification on Nuclear Power systems, Radiation control and handling, Cryogenics, and shipboard Mega Diesel.

After discharge from the Navy, John and his brother started a new company and developed it into sales exceeding $5 million annually. This Chicago-based tank farm and processing plant encompassed a fleet of semi-trucks and tankers, a large fleet of tug boats and barges, and an ocean cargo ship based in Houston.

With the creativeness of his brother, the realtor, and the banker, John purchased his first the house with no money down (and a bad credit score). This was the first property of many he acquired through creative processes. John started buying up HUD listed properties, fixing and reselling them, and held multiple projects at one time. He was successful at it until the dissolution of the partnership. By this time, he had personally acquired multiple multi-unit apartment buildings specializing on two-flats.

John has also been involved with tax sales, land development, and options selling. His dream is the development of 100-unit senior living communities with 24hour in-house medical staffing. With these huge aspirations, John researched and found formal real estate education to be prepared for the large scale investor projects that lay ahead in his career.

Shannon:
What inspired you to get into real estate?

John:
My desire for real estate goes all the way back to my parents. My mother and father were hardworking, Midwestern, blue collar workers. My Mom was a nurse, a seamstress, and she was even a published author. She wrote some books and a lot of short stories that were published in all the women's magazines. She usually did all that at the same time.

My father was a dairy farmer, and after we left the farm, he got a job at the school district as a custodian. I grew up understanding hard work and how important it was to honor your word.

But what my parents couldn't teach me is how to own my own property. They were renters, they were always renters. We always looked up to property owners and landlords, and I grew up thinking that property ownership was only for a select few—the elite. I always had respect for property owners, and that was a huge burn down deep inside of me—to eventually become part of that elite group. I never was able to acquire the skills of being a real estate owner through my parents, but that's where I got my drive and love of it.

Shannon:

If someone was going to get started in real estate, what would you rec-ommend they do first?

John:

First thing is learn your 'why.' At some point, you will hit some type of wall. You're going to have problems where it is so easy to give up. Right then, you're going to have to dig down deep inside yourself. Find out what is that burn down deep inside that makes you step out of your comfort zone to do that extra thing? What drives you to pick up that scary phone and talk to a stranger about setting an appointment to see his house he needs to sell? Is it your boss that gets paid so much more than you and getting the credit for your work? Is it that you're almost 50 and you don't have enough retirement for you to ever stop working? Is it that you your kids are in high school and you have no idea how to pay for their college? You got to figure out what your 'why' is.

Then you need to figure out what are your strengths and weak-nesses. Write them on a piece of paper and be honest with yourself. Under your strengths column, find ways to build upon them. Under your weaknesses column, find ways to overcome them. By me giving myself an honest self-assessment, I have converted those weaknesses into new strengths. I became a successful Investor because of things that used to be my weaknesses, but through understanding myself I was able to make them my strongest strengths. I was always uncom-fortable starting a conversation with a stranger. Now at every property I go inspect, I make it a point to walk around until I see a neighbor and ask them everything possible about the neighborhood and the prop-erty. Because of me overcoming that fear of starting a conversation with a stranger, that new strength has lead me to find many more real estate deals and has prevented me from making many bad decisions.

Shannon:

So, if someone wanted to get started in real estate, but they had very little money or poor credit, what are some strategies that they could use to get into real estate investing?

John:

To answer this, let me explain how I got started. I got out of the Navy and after returning home from the military, I was newly divorced, my credit was shot, and my total life savings could fit comfortably in my wallet. One day, I was driving down the street and passed a two-flat. I saw that it had some fire damage, and it had a "For Sale" sign out front. I was curious so I made the call. Three weeks later I ended up buying that two-flat, and the two-flat right next door to it. The owner was having some problems with the city and was unable to attain a permit to repair the damage. He had some pain and was looking for opportunity to resolve his pain. He personally financed both units along with most of the money used for repairs. He was an Investor and understood how to structure this. I had no credit, no money, and I ended up buying two properties, two-flats, with only $2,000 down. He never ran a credit check, and I never got a bank involved.

You don't need good credit. You really don't even need a lot of money to be able to get started. What you need is the ability to go out and ask the right questions—pick up the phone and call the number on the "For Sale by Owner" sign. There are opportunities out there. Having good credit, having stable income and a big nest egg in the bank is great—I didn't have any of that. I built everything I have today off of those (2) fire-burnout two-flats. It was my start in real estate investing which has led to a strong passive income—all because this gentleman had some pain and I solved it for him.

Shannon:

You said he turned out to be one of your mentors. How have mentors in your real estate investing helped you navigate different or other potential pitfalls?

John:

This gentleman had some real estate problems. I helped solve those problems. He became my mentor because I had no idea what I was doing (both of us understood that). I remember that we were sitting at the table closing on the first of the two-flats that he was selling me. I looked across the table, I said, "I can fix these buildings, but after I get them fixed up, how do I find a good tenant?" He just looked at me and said, "John, when you're talking to the applicant and you think that they're going to be a good tenant for you, after they fill out the application and everything looks to be fine, walk them to their car. Be very casual about it but look at their car. Does it have duct tape holding the bumper on? Are the tires bald and no maintenance has ever been done to it? Look inside and see if it is full of McDonald's and Burger King trash." He said, "A person will maintain their automobile like they maintain their home. If they respect their automobile, they will respect their home." I found that to be true test about 90 percent of the time. I use that every time I screen a tenant. This of course isn't the only thing I look for—they have to pass a background and credit check—but it does give me a little insight to how responsible they are for their belongings. Mentors have taught me little things in my business that have made all the difference. A little nugget like that could lead you down a path that you wouldn't have went down, or lead you away from a path that you were dead set on going on that would've been disastrous. If a mentor tells you to go look at somebody's car as part of your screening process, then go look at their car. A true mentor has your best interest at heart, so they will help guide if you listen. Use their knowledge to grow yours.

Shannon:
If someone wanted to invest in multi-family units like you do, what advice would you give them?

John:
The first mistake an amateur investor makes is they treat a rental like a home that they're going to be living in. If you're going to live in it, then you fix it one way. If it's going to be a rental, then figure out what the area will support. If you're in a class-C property, (which are the properties that I love investing in), and all the rest of the rentals have Formica countertops and prefabbed cabinets from the big box home owners lumber yards, for instance, then you don't want to have high-end cabinets and high-grade quartz countertops. You might think it's the greatest kitchen in the world after putting in all that

money and labor to get it perfect, but you can't support it economically. There will be no Return on Investment for those upgrades, and the tenant moving in would have been just as happy with the Ikea or Menards cabinets. Don't put your desires into that unit; figure out what is customary in that specific target rental area and put those repairs in.

Now, I always like to upgrade a little from that base line. I like to put a little bit nicer things in, but I always keep in mind what the area will actually support for a rental. Where is my ROI? What are people expecting to find when they walk into a rental in that neighborhood, and I give just a bit more. I do this to shorten my vacancy rate.

When doing a kitchen rehab, I put in IKEA kitchen cabinets. When an applicant is inspecting the house, they always open the kitchen cabinets because they look a little different. When they see the steel sides on the drawers, and the way they sit above the floor on feet, they start imagining themselves with their things in those drawers. I've rented a lot of my units because of those cabinets. Things like that will also get a conversation started. By taking that extra couple of minutes talking about the cabinets, it always leads to other topics. This is where you start building a relationship with this person and find out what type of person they may actually be.

Shannon:
Did you say class-C properties—can you explain why you like them?

John:
At this point I still manage my own properties. I strategically invested in a specific area so all my units are within just a couple of minutes of one another and it's easy to manage. I understand my investor ID and know that I am comfortable dealing with that class of property. My class C properties are all in lower-middle income areas. A few of my units are Section 8 and some are affiliated with the Veterans Assistance programs. I try to keep a portion of my portfolio in subsidized units. I still screen those applicants the same, and I have had great subsidized tenants. It's all about the person—not if they are getting assistance or not.

Shannon:
What is an investor ID?

John:
An investor ID is assessing who you are and what you're comfortable doing. When you did your self-assessment looking for your strengths and weaknesses, you should have realized what direction in real estate investing you are most able to succeed at. You have to understand what your strategies are. If you are really good at fixing something up, and you want to be a part of a fix and flip, where you just fix it up and you sell it, then that is your ID. If you are a shopper and always find great deals, but you don't really want to deal with tenants, then you might want to look at wholesaling as your ID. If you are after passive income and dream of owning a lot of property that is paying for itself and your retirement, then a Buy and Hold could possibly be your ID. If that is you but you're not comfortable dealing with tenants directly and telling them that they are late on the rent, trying to figure out how to deal with a property issue—then your ID would not to manage yourself and use a professional management company to manage your rentals. You have to assess what you're comfortable with, and that's what a buyer ID does. It assesses who you are and what you're going to be the most successful doing. Don't do something that you're not comfortable with because you're not going to be good at it. If you're not good at it, you're not going to be successful and profitable

Shannon:
How does real estate allow you to earn passive and massive income?

John:
Isn't that what real estate investing is all about? Being educated enough to earn passive or massive income? I really think this topic should be taught in school. To be able to have passive and massive income, you have to be a problem solver. You have to be a real estate pain remover.

When I had a W-2 job, I was approached by one of my employees. He had a problem and needed to sell his property. He needed

$15,000 fast to help him relocate. It had an old mobile home on it, but it had a really nice lot. The trailer was unsalvageable but I bought it because I saw potential. I didn't have it in cash, but I had a credit card that was paid off and it had a $20,000 limit. I charged all of his moving expenses on my credit card. I ended up finding somebody that needed the frame of the trailer, so I demolished the trailer and sold him the frame. I got enough from the frame to cover the cost of the demo and the dumpster.

I found somebody else that had a really nice late model mobile home that had to move it off the property where it was parked. I moved that really nice trailer onto this lot. Within just a few days of purchasing the property, I had a really nice 3-bedroom 2-bathroom trailer set up on a beautiful lot. I put a "For Rent" sign out front. In two days, I had somebody call and offer me cash to sell it to them. I made $41,000 dollars on that property. I fixed three people's problems, and made $41,000 in the process in just a few days.

An entry level position as a policeman or a local fireman would have made less money in a year than what I made on that one property in just a few days. All I did was I fixed a couple of people's problems.

My first two flats that I bought from the distressed Investor, I gave him $35,000 for each unit. He also gave me an extra loan to cover the cost of repairs. He personally held the mortgages on them so I never had to deal with a bank. I had $60,000 in one, $55,000 in the other after repairs. My loan payments plus taxes and insurance were around $850 a month per unit. I rented each apartment out for $900 a month times 4 units. So, in the end, my passive cash flow ended up to be about $1,900 a month, after expenses.

My first fix and flip I made $100,000. I lived in the house while I renovated it, so I counted all the money that I put into repairs as rent because I'd have to pay that money I was using for repairs to somebody else as rent

So, by just driving by that fire damaged two-flat with a sign out front, I made $1,900 a month passive income. From solving those three people's problems on that trailer deal, I made $41,000 in 10 days. To the policeman or to the fireman who put themselves in harm's way every day, $41,000 on one quick real estate transaction is massive. It just depends on what your opinion is on massive. Massive income is relative—what do you think massive really is? Maybe it's just $1500 to get your car fixed or an extra $200 a month to pay for braces for your son.

Shannon:

So how does running multiple investing strategies protect and accelerate your investing success?

John:

If you know only one method of investment, then you'll always be trying to fit everything into that method even if it doesn't fit. It could be like driving a round peg into a square hole. By having the education of multiple strategies and how they may interact together, you're going to be able solve more problems, and you're going to have greater profits. Remember that being a successful real estate investor is becoming a problem solver. If you're a professional problem solver you're going to be a really good Investor. Every real estate transaction is different; some will fit with just one technique perfectly but some are more complex and need a blend of different methods to work. Those are the deals that usually have bigger profits when all the pieces fit together. So, understand that when you find a deal that is perfect but you don't know how to structure it, you may need to blend a few different techniques together to make it work for all parties.

Shannon:

You touched a little bit on cash flow on your first two properties. What is cash flow, and why is it important?

John:

Cash flow pays the bills. You have household expenses and so does your business, so you need some type of income. Cash flow takes care of all of those expenses. After the monthly expenses are covered, you can start living the life you want. You can even live the life you dream about. Unlike a W-2 employee, where you're stuck with "X" amount of dollars a month, you're an entrepreneur, so go find someone to help and create more income. If you're a real estate investor, and you're not living the life that you want, you go find another deal. Go help somebody solve a problem. There are people everywhere that are struggling to find the answer—so be that problem solver. Cash flow is just based on the amount of people that you help.

Shannon:
How long have you been doing real estate investing? For how many years?

John:
I've been doing it for 30 years. I started as soon as I got out of the US Navy. With my brother's help, I bought my first rehab fix and flip.

Shannon:
So you've seen the economy go up and down.

John:
Yes, the economy has great growth cycles and then times of correction. I had a lot of investments out there when the market crashed in 2006–2009 but didn't have the education and skills to see that as a great opportunity. I was like the masses and saw it as an end to my investment portfolio.

Shannon:
Is real estate investing success dependent on a strong economy?

John:
No. If you have different strategies in your arsenal, then the condition of the economy has got nothing to do with it. Actually, a weaker economy will give you more opportunity. Some strategies are better suited in a growing and strong economy, and some will do better in a falling or failing economy. For instance, if the interest rates are climbing, and it's going into a slower economy, you may find the perfect situation to use a 'subject to' or seller finance strategy and

use the existing mortgage that is in place where the interest rate is lower than it is today.

You need a wide range of real estate investment techniques to be able to weather any economy out. Because remember, the profit in the deal depends on when you buy the property, not when you sell it. So, if you buy it in one economy, and you try to sell it in the other, and you made a good decision when you bought it, you're still profitable no matter what the economy is.

Shannon:
What is a 'subject to'?

John:
'Subject to' transactions are when you help a seller by buying their property but leaving their existing mortgage in place. You cover all expenses and have ownership of the property but the seller still holds the original mortgage in their name. If a property is purchased on a 'subject to' strategy and you pay $100,000 at 7 percent for 20 years but the seller owes the bank $50,000 at 5 percent and still has 20 years left on the original 30-year mortgage, then the seller actually makes 2 percent on the $50,000 that the bank is owed. That's over $10,000 of income they made on just the bank's money. The seller also shows the transaction as income so it reflects the transaction as an investment and has little effect normally on their ability to attain any new credit.

When you sit down with somebody and you show them the math, and explain what their tax liability is because of depreciation, their capital gains exposure and what they're going to make on interest keeping the mortgage in place, it becomes a simple decision for the seller. You solve their real estate problem, defer their capital gains exposure into the future, and you give them an increase in their interest rate to be able to help compensate for that tax debt. Now of course this is just a simplified example—you normally have to blend a couple of strategies into this to make it a win for the seller, a win for the mortgage holder, a win for the IRS and a WIN for you. I love this strategy because it solves problems that so many people are having today.

Shannon:

How do you minimize that risk of investing so that you can maximize success?

John:

One of the things I'm the proudest of is I've never lost a dollar on any real estate transaction I've ever done. I don't know why, because in my earlier real estate purchases I didn't have the skills that I have today. It was just pure luck that I never lost any money. I put the deals together the best I could. I thought they were good deals, so I dug in and made them all work. I realized that I was smart enough to put deals together, but I also was smart enough that I understood I was leaving a lot of money on the table. Money that was mine, if I asked for it, if I structured the deal right, if I went to a different source for lending.

Education is the key. It wasn't until recently that I received the education that has made a huge impact in my business. I could have been so much more profitable with the skills that I have acquired in the last couple of years. With the education system that I've been exposed to and some of the things that I've learned, I would have seen all of those missed opportunities that were in front of me but just lying under the surface for me to reach in and grab. So many times, I veered away from a huge opportunity because I didn't have the skills to understand how to structure them. To answer your question on how to minimize risk and maximize success you need to get a proper real estate investment education. It took me years to find one that gave me what I need, and I now am growing my portfolio weekly because of it.

Shannon:

In your business, how do you help others learn more about real estate?

John:

Right now, I am concentrating a lot of my efforts on financial literacy. I am guiding others in how to invest by showing them what I've done and how I've done it. I'm explaining to groups of people how I've been able to make the deals that I've done, and how I've structured things. There are certain trainings that I love to show others that gives them the idea that a W-2 position is not a death sentence and that there are things that they can do today to start working to the point of never needing that 'job' again.

I've got a local group that I actually take around and do little mini neighborhood tours. I get a big shuttle bus van and I'll fill it full of people. I'll drive into a neighborhood I'm familiar with, and I'll show them how to find a potential profitable property. They learn what properties that I think could be obtained and why. After taking down a bunch of addresses, we go into the conference room and I sit down in front of the computer. I show them how to find the owners, how to find the correct parcel numbers, and get all the pertinent information that an investor really needs. We find out how to contact the owner of the property. How to talk to the owner after they respond and to get them to says "Yes, I might be interested in selling it." Then how to talk to that person during the property showing. I try to convey my knowledge of the 30 years that I've been buying and selling properties, to anybody that is serious about learning about how become an investor, it excites me to see someone make an offer on their first investment property.

Shannon:
What are some other creative ways that you would use to acquire properties?

John:
The first couple investment properties I did were seller financed. An investor owned those buildings mortgage free, and he needed to do something with them. He knew that my credit was bad. Basically, what I had in my life fit in my wallet. I didn't have anything. There was no way that I would ever qualify for a conventional loan on two rental units. He understood that to be able to make the deal work for both of us, he had to hold the mortgages on them. I've done a few of those, where I found the right seller that had no loan or mortgage on the property. They were looking at the benefits of holding the mortgage themselves and collecting

the interest. Those sellers were more interested in passive income than the lump sum cash. That goes back to you finding out what pain or what problems the person on the other side of the table is having and how you're going to solve them. You do that by asking a lot of questions.

As much as I like owner finance, I like 'subject to' deals. There is only a small percentage of real estate owners who own the property clear of any liens. Most have some type of mortgage on them. 'Subject to' is a great strategy to master. If the seller doesn't need the entire balance of the property in a lump sum payment, then a 'subject to' may work well for them. Find out what they really need out of the deal and solve their problem.

Shannon:

So John, the reason I'm asking this question is you talked about how you'll get in the van and you'll fill it with people and go look at property. So that's really creative. Very few real estate investors I have heard of actually use that. Now there are some people that will go out and say I look for tall grass, I look for this, I look for that. So when you're not filling up your 15-passenger van, what are some other ways that you search for, or that you look for, in properties that are kind of creative and kind of out of the box?

John:

Well, for a while I was looking at media like Craigslist and online local papers. I also look at the online auction sites. I found a couple of opportunities, but I don't like fighting over the same property with everyone else. I like finding my properties before others even know they're available. The most luck I'm having right now are from networking events. There's a lot of networking groups out there. There are Meet-Ups, there's Chamber of Commerce groups, there are all types of real estate groups. Go and start looking for a group to meet and possibly join. You will find by attending a few meetings at one group, it will open the door to a few more and possibly better groups. Most of them will be very welcoming to real estate investors. If they understand that you're not trying to take advantage of their members and that you're trying to go and find people to help, then they will share info with you and you will run into a lot of great property opportunities. I go into these networking groups and I explain that I am a real estate investor and educator, how can I help the group?

Sometimes they just ask me to do a little training or to share some of my experiences. I've been able to explain how some of the processes work that I've used and some of the things that I've done. Networking groups are amazing. They are very open to different exposures and knowledge that will help their community.

Shannon:

What do you think is the number one mistake that an individual makes when buying their first investment property?

John:

Well there's two. The biggest mistake an Investor is going to make is not thinking they have what it takes to do it. So they never even get started. They worry about the financing, their credit score, their ability to make it work. They haven't found their 'why.' I'm talking about the 'why' that drives them. If they have found that burn down deep, then that fear of the unknown is just a squeak that is easy to ignore.

The next thing is a new investor always tries to treat their rental properties like it's their home—It's not, it's a rental property. Understand what market you're in, and what people are going to expect when they come to your property. Give them a little better than their expectations. Don't go crazy on the landscaping or the amenities unless it is required to conform to the other rentals of that type in your market. You're not going to be living there so treat it like the rental unit that it is. Everything you do, think of the Return on Investment. If it doesn't make sense to put in glass kitchen cabinet doors, then why are you wanting to install them?

Shannon:

What advice would you give someone that has something holding them back from starting a real estate investment career?

John:

Things that hold people back are fear. If fear is controlling you, it's going to limit your ability to function efficiently.

Shannon:

I come to you and I say: "I really want to do what you do. But I've got a great job, I've got a family that depends on me, and I'm just scared."

John:

I just heard this recently, and I wish I knew who said it. "Any decision made in fear is likely to be wrong." Find out what the root of your fear is and solve it. Dig down deep and find that burn that keeps you going when you want to quit, and that 'why' will overcome your fear. That 'why' will help you take that first step. It's just that little first step. It's not that big. Take the first step, the 'why' will help you do that. Then it will help you take a second step, then another. All of the sudden, the fear isn't loud.

Shannon:

What type of legacy do you want to leave?

John:

My legacy is more than how comfortable I leave my family. I will of course have retirement accounts running for my grandchildren so they will have the ability to use those funds for higher education or investments. Those accounts will have rental properties running in them to build long running passive income.

I want to leave a legacy of how people knew me, how they remember me. I want people telling my family how I've helped them when they had problems. People that had real estate issues and they didn't know how to solve them. Families that didn't know how to move on with their life and they reached out and I helped them. There are a lot of people on that list already but there is room for a lot more.

I want to have people say that before they met me they weren't able to buy their first home. They didn't have the credit—they didn't have the skills—they didn't have 20 percent—or they didn't have that other thing that prevented them from living their dream. Then they got introduced to me, and I helped them put a deal together where the structure worked for everybody. Their family was then able to buy their first home. When they come to sign the paperwork, their kids are running through the house picking out whose bedroom is whose. I've always liked that sound as the kids argue on who gets which room. It gives me that warm and fuzzy feeling and makes me feel good. I've got two of those deals happening right now, where the family have not been able to get their own home. As an investor, I am able to see things that the big banks don't see. I understand who they are and why their credit score is low. A problem that happened years ago that was a life altering event doesn't always dictate who they are today.

That issue that screwed up their record, really isn't who they are today. As an investor, I'm able to see past that and put a deal in place. I'm giving these families an opportunity to buy their first home and live that American Dream of home ownership. It may seem corny but when someone is getting their first house after believing that it will never happen, they will fight hard to keep it—they will do just about anything to keep their family in that home. There is a huge mindset difference from a tenant to a home owner. Those are the kind of legacies I want to leave. People remembering me for those kinds of actions.

The people that I've helped out of a problem when they didn't know where else to go and the first-time home buyers. That's why I do what I do. The passive income is amazing and it has changed my life. My family at first didn't understand why I would give up the security of corporate America but now enjoys that I have the time freedom most people never see. I do keep extremely busy but it is on tasks I choose to do, not assignments a boss at a job I hate has given me to do. What drives me now is helping others—solving people's problems. This path is also leading me down a path of passive income and strong financial security. My family will have financial security for generations to come from the work I'm doing today.

Patrick & Paul McCrimmon

Patrick & Paul Enterprises Inc. was founded in 2007 with the purchase of their first three rental properties. Patrick McCrimmon and Paul McCrimmon are award winning real estate investors who now have over 30 rental properties, have fixed and flipped over 35 single family homes in the Chicago land area and have produced double digit returns for their investors.

Paul has a Bachelor of science degree from Elmhurst College in Computer Science. With over 30 years of experience in Information technology, Paul brings attentions to detail, strong organizational skills, strong procedural and leadership skills to the company.

Patrick has a Bachelor of Arts degree from DePaul University with a concentration in Information Technology. With 30 years of experience in Information Technology, Patrick brings attention to detail, and strong organizational, communication, leadership, and team building skills to the company.

Patrick and Paul have a very strong commitment to their families, their investors and the real estate investment community. They work directly with new real estate investors, sharing their knowledge and experience, so the new real estate investors can build their own successful real estate business.

Patrick enjoys teaching taekwondo to children at the local park district. He enjoys traveling with his family throughout the United States and Europe. Patrick has been married 32 years and has 3 grown children.

Paul enjoys traveling throughout the United States and spending time with his grandchildren. Paul has been married 35 years and has 2 grown children.

Shannon:

I hear quite a bit about brothers going into business together but also being identical twins has to add to the experience. Being twins has to make the experience even better.

Patrick:

It has. The biggest difference we see in being twins is that there is no real older sibling. Yes, I am two minutes older but in reality, that doesn't count. We make our decisions on committee and try to stay on track with what is best for both of us. When we work together we always have a great time whether it is painting an apartment or finding our next fix and flip.

We do have many of the same interests. We both went into computers over 30 years ago and created some great careers. However, we also had the same faults in when we hit 50 we both realized we had not put enough money away for retirement. We both hold the same belief that the baby-boomers in front of us will significantly change both Medicare and social security by either bankrupting it or significantly reducing it to almost nothing. Paul had mentioned a couple of times about going into real estate but I did not listen. I was fine as an Information Technology Project Lead for the company I was working for. Finally, in 2007, Paul convinced me to buy some rentals for tax deduction purposes and we did. We purchased three rental properties. If we knew then what we know now we would have never purchased those properties.

Shannon:

So, 2007 is when you finally got him to join on, and what a horrible year to start real estate.

Patrick:

We know.

Shannon:

Well, and so, Patrick, that's how you got started. Paul, it seems like you were inspired to get into real estate investing sooner than Patrick was, so what inspired you? Why did you want to get into real estate investing?

Paul:

I had looked at multiple ways to increase my income many times. I tried a few inventions, and I bought some training tapes. I even tried doing some direct sales of water filter systems and selling high end vacuum cleaners. I went to a couple real estate seminars but these businesses and ideas just did not seem to go anywhere.

In 2007, I don't know exactly why but Pat agreed to buy a couple rentals. We were coming up on our 50th birthday and had hardly anything put away for retirement. We also had children either in college or getting ready to go soon. We had to do something and knew that almost all the wealthy people own real estate.

Shannon:

So, Pat...

Patrick:

We bought three houses in 2007, all rental properties. All the wrong way. I mean, they basically cash-flowed a very small amount of money every month.

We, like many uneducated investors at that time, bought them for tax write-offs and appreciation. Unfortunately, the very next year I had a life change. The company I worked for began doing layoffs like many other companies at that time. On March 17, 2008, my job went to India, and I went to the unemployment line. I was there for over 13 years, but some of the other people who also were laid off were there for over 20 years. They gave me a nice severance package but I looked for another job for eight months. I took a job that paid 60 percent of what I was making. I began to look very seriously at starting a business. I was now forced to do something because every month we spent more than we made. I had to do something before I lost everything.

Patrick:

I looked into buying a franchise but each one required a very large startup cost with a very small return. Many times taking five to ten years to get your return on the investment.

Paul:

We realized how little we knew about being real estate investors when we went to get a mortgage on our fourth house and were declined. We had great incomes and very high credit scores but still were denied. We did not know why, but we did know we needed to find a better way to do real estate to be successful.

Shannon:

Okay. How many times did you ask Pat if he wanted to invest in real estate? So, Paul, you asked Pat three times, 2001, 2000-whatever, and 2007?

Paul:

I remember at least three times. Once in 2001, again in 2004, and then again in 2007.

Shannon:

So, Pat, why did you decide yes in 2007? What was different about the way he asked? What changed in your life, or what inspired you in 2007 to go ahead and get involved?

Patrick:

Taxes. Both my wife and I had good jobs and decent incomes, but we were paying a lot to Uncle Sam. Real estate seemed like a great way to keep more money in my pocket. My wife was working over half the year just to give the money to the government. I wanted a way to keep more of the money. I had never been anything but a W2 employee, but real estate seemed like something I could do. Besides when we started Paul did most of the work.

Paul found the houses. They were close to his house in an area we both knew very well. We expected the houses to appreciate in value. We would have business expenses, depreciation, and many other write-offs to our taxes.

Shannon:
Right. How'd that work out for you?

Patrick:
We got bitten.

Patrick:
Yeah. The tax advantages kind of went away when the job went away.

Shannon:
Wow.

Patrick:
Which I understood; the company was dependent of the housing market. With the collapse of that market they had to lower their expenses to stay in business. The company did some of this by sending jobs like mine overseas. It helped their budget but was devastating to mine. I now understood what was meant by the most dangerous thing to your economic success was having only one income. I will never be solely dependent on one company of one income stream ever again. I have seen too many friends lose everything because they lost that one income stream.

I was very desperate then; I was unemployed, and I had to start over again. This was not my first layoff, but the major difference was my children were now college age or close to it and I was in my 50s. I did not have enough money to retire either and between 2001-2005 and 2007, my 401k had become 101k.

Paul:

And that was one of the selling points, too, when I talked to Pat. We were looking at our jobs and our current situation. I too had been laid off a couple of times prior to that. So we're looking at these jobs going, "Um, you know." My job had been sent overseas a couple times on me, too. So we looked and had the realization there is no such thing anymore as "job security." There is only the corporate bottom line. We needed something that's going to make it through what could be 30 or more years of retirement. My mother lived to 94 and my father-in-law is now in his late 80s. That's a long time and requires a great deal of retirement income. As Pat said earlier, we don't trust Social Security or Medicare and don't want to retire waiting each month for a small social security check. We do fix and flips to create the money to buy rental properties. Those rental properties will be our retirement income. We are going to be responsible for future and not rely on the small hand-outs from social security.

And that's pretty much the selling point that I used on him. And then he says, "Okay. We both need to make it through retirement." So we decided at that point it was time to start looking at real estate.

We only had one problem. Neither of us knew anything about how to do real estate. We are the sixth and seventh of eight children of 8 in a W2 family. We were in IT for 30 years. Neither Pat nor I knew much about being real estate investors.

Shannon:

Perfect.

Patrick:

One more thing I'd like to add was that Paul and I had talked many, many years ago about how we had no belief in the Social Security system and Medicare, and if it will even be anything with the Baby Boomers that are in front of us. I mean, we are part of the Baby Boomers, but we are at the end of it, so there is disbelief in that program even existing for us.

My major fear was at that time, being 52, was the idea that it was going to be either "Welcome to Walmart" or "Would you like fries with that" that was going to be my retirement.

Shannon:
Yeah. Try being a Gen-Xer.

Patrick:
Yeah. I thought that's where I was going to be in my 70s. That was not my plan.

Shannon:
So how had your education in real estate changed the way that you invest?

Patrick:
Paul, I'll let you take this one.

Paul:
The education helped us with focus and direction. We used the strategies we learned to build a proper business model. Create focus on what we needed to do to create the type of business that would generate the income we need now and for retirement. With the education, we were able to make good, conscious, knowledgeable decisions on exactly what we were going to do.

So the education helped us put together a strategy, helped us with buying and doing the kind of properties that we wanted to do. And also, I mean, when we got the education, we grabbed that education, we used it right away, and within six months we had made four times the cost of that education as income.

So the education was actually one of the cheapest things we did, but it also helped us be able to make knowledgeable decisions about our business and how to run it, and how to actually make money at it.

Shannon:
Nice. So, Paul, you actually said the education helped you figure out creative ways to find what kind of properties you want to do.

Paul:
Yes. Our main focus has been REO properties for both fix and flips and rentals, but we have bought a few short sales and we even did

one master lease of a single-family home where the owner was going to Texas for two years and needed someone to take care of his house while he was away. We leased his house and then sub-leased it to a tenant. We paid his mortgage, taxes, and other expenses with the rent. Our income was the difference between the rent we collected and the expenses. It was great because it did not cost us anything and we helped out the homeowner. Two years later he returned to his house.

One of our favorite acquisition strategies we learned is online auctions. We have purchased many houses through online auctions.

Shannon:
So do you guys always agree on the type of properties that you want to do?

Patrick:
When we first started flipping doing real estate after buying those three houses, we got together and created a business plan to define our strengths and our weaknesses, our time and resource limitations. We then discussed which allocation strategy worked best for us and the type of houses we would buy as fix and flips and the types of rental properties we would buy. We buy light rehab, newer first time and one upper homes in the western suburbs of Chicago. We sometimes disagreed on the value of the house and the cost of the repairs. We learned how important it was to do our own evaluations and have information to support the numbers we came up with.

Paul:
There have been a couple of disagreements with other people; you know, we would look at a house and disagree on how much it is worth in its current condition. The realtor or the bank or the wholesaler would say the property is worth a certain amount and we would look at it and the comparables and ask them if they would personally pay that much for the house. We would negotiate back and forth until we got our price or we walked away. As I have learned, it's better to walk away from a deal than to buy a bad deal.

Patrick:

We have strayed from our business plan a couple of times and bought some fantastic older homes, but for the most part, we keep within that business plan, and that way we knew exactly what we're looking for and we knew exactly what type of houses we want.

We've went out of our investing area a couple of times for some great deals but, for the most part, because we built that business plan, it's made it easier for us to be partners and to stay on track.

Shannon:

Yeah. It sounds like your core business strategy you could agree on. And the only thing that you would disagree would be really opinions, but your facts seem like they're all in line; is that an accurate statement?

Patrick:

That is.

Paul:

Yes.

Shannon:

Perfect. So what is your favorite type of property to do or what is in your business plan? Are we talking about fix-and-flips, are we talking about buy-and-holds, are we talking about 'subject-to,' short-sales? What do you guys like to do?

Patrick:

Our major focus is long term income so our focus is buy-and-holds. The strategy we use is fix and flips to get the money we need to either buy outright or finance a buy-and-hold property. So what we're actually after is not massive income, it is actually passive income. That is our business plan is to build passive income. Many of our fix and flips were built since 1990.

Shannon:

Really?

Patrick:

Yes. The types of houses we look for must have at least three bedrooms, one-and-a-half bathrooms, a two-car garage, and a basement. This is our basic model we look to purchase. We buy these because we are not heavy duty, lifelong construction people. We don't have the skills or knowledge necessary to do major rehabs. This was identified as one of our weakness so we only do newer homes.

We do first-time home buyer homes, and one-uppers, so second homes. And so we generally look for a house that will resell for between $150,000 and $350,000. Those are in different areas; in some areas $150,000 is a first-time home buyer home and in other areas $350,000 is a first-time home buyer home. Nonetheless, they fit our business model. This is where the largest percentage of the home buyers in our area buy homes. Those are the families we target.

We like to say that we take damaged non-performing properties and return them into beautiful family homes. We make money doing this but it is a service that is needed by the banks, investment firms, and families. We are proud of our fix and flip properties and the kind of work we do.

My favorite experience is sitting at the closing table when we are selling a house to a new homeowner and watching their excitement when I give them the key to their new home. It is priceless.

Our rental properties have a different business description. Many times they're a little bit older homes in a working-class neighborhood, which is kind of where we came from. We came from a working-class neighborhood. So we're very comfortable working and negotiating and talking and relating to our tenants. We buy rental properties that also need repair. Both single family homes and small multi-units. We then fix them up and turn them into nice rentals.

A few years back we purchased an ugly house in Sandwich, Illinois. Our contractors even said it was ugly. Then they started to work on it. Paint the interior and the exterior, replace some windows, install a drain tile, trim the trees, put down new gravel in the driveway. When it was done, the contractors said they really liked the house. Purchased for $30,000, put $15,000 of repairs into it, and then rented them out for $1,300 a month. That's a great rental and a wonder house. Four years later the tenant bought the house.

Shannon:

Have you had a bedroom/bathroom minimum on your rentals?

Patrick:

We base our rental more on cash flow then on physical characteristics. In our area the better rental houses have at least three bedrooms, one and a half baths and a two-car garage. Those are the easiest to rent but we do have some rental houses which are smaller.

Shannon:

Do they have to have a basement?

Patrick:

We are about half and half. The ones that do not have basements are in an area where basement are not common. Basements are good because they are easier to rent but we have found they are not required.

Shannon:

So where are you guys located that you find enough homes with basements?

Patrick:

For fix and flips basements are almost required. A lot of houses will not sell unless they have a basement. Of course, a lot of houses won't sell unless they have a two-car garage either.

Shannon:

So if you are starting with very little money or poor credit, what are some strategies that you can use to get started in real estate?

Paul:

I have to tell you that I did start with no money. I have had a great career with a better than I ever expected salary but at the same time I, like many people, kept putting off saving for retirement till later. Because I had great income I did have great credit.

But back to your question. Without money or credit, you need to build a list of people you know who might have money or credit you could borrow. Real estate investing requires money but it doesn't have to be your money. You then create a business plan to show the potential investor. You then go find a deal. You then present each of the investors with the deal and most likely one of them will be interested.

The other way to start is to become a wholesaler. Find properties for fix and flippers or buy-and-holders. If you find a property and negotiate a good deal you can then assign the contract to another real estate investor and get paid. Wholesaling doesn't require any of your own cash and they don't look at your credit. You must be able to find good deals for your buyers. This is a great way to get started making money and getting into real estate. Buyers like great wholesalers and will pay you to find them great real estate deals.

You must gain people's trust especially if you expect them to invest in your deal. You must create a relationship and you must keep your word. These are expected, but I would like to add one more. When something doesn't go as planned, a buyer walks away, a house doesn't sell as expected, you must also communicate this information to the investor too. The worst thing to do is leave your investor guessing.

Patrick:

One of the main points that came through for me was if you want people to invest in your real estate deal you must ask them. You must tell your friends, co-workers, church members about your business and income opportunity. You never know who has money and is willing to invest in you.

I was talking to one of my neighbors once about my business and the money I was paying my investors. A few weeks later they gave me $150,000 for a real estate deal I was doing. Four months later I gave them back their money and $15,000 in interest. I asked them what made them decide to invest in the deal. They told me their daughter was getting married the next year, and they saw it as an opportunity to get some money to pay for the wedding. I thought that was awesome. It was like free money for the wedding.

Shannon:

How do you find those people? Because as you said, "Some of the people you wouldn't expect to have money or you wouldn't think would have money." Do you just walk up to them and say, "Hey, so I want to invest in real estate, do you have any money?"

Patrick:

No. We are a bit less direct. We started by talking about the deal and then started talking how much money the investor was going to make in the deal. We also explain how the money would be secured by both the real estate and insurance. Then we would ask if they knew anyone who might be interested in the deal.

After we did a few houses, investors started walking up to us asking if we could use their money to do deals. I did not believe this when I first heard it but it is true. Money will come if you have good deals, run your business as a professional, and always keep your word.

Paul:

A lot of times we talked about our current investor, we would talk about how well we were taking care of that person, making them really happy, and the returns they were making on their money. That person would tell someone else or they themselves would say they were not happy with their current returns and want to give us some money for our deals. I have been offered hundreds of thousands of dollars by people I did not expect to have that kind of money. You never know if you don't tell people what you're doing.

Shannon:

Wow, that's awesome.

Paul:

Some of our investors have only done one deal, but our original investors have stayed with us for years. They are retired or about to retire and want a better than CD or IRA return on their retirement. They understand that even though they are no longer working their money must continue to grow. They need a very low risk investment with a high return to maintain their standard of living through their retirement decades. We explain to our investors that our strategy is to always pay our investors first. Our investors never lose money, that's part of our business plan.

Shannon:
Well, that's a wise plan that makes people want to invest with you.

Paul:
Yeah.

Shannon:
In fact, that may actually be part of the answer to this next question: what is the number one mistake an individual makes when buying their first investment property?

Paul:
Paying too much or doing unnecessary repairs. This happens when the person is too eager to do a deal verses a good deal. Either they do sloppy calculations or they change the calculations to make the deal look better than it really is. They fall in love with the deal instead of the numbers.

A house is an investment in your business and must be treated as one. It is a means to an end. Don't fall in love with the house, fall in love with the numbers and the income the house will create. If you look at the numbers and the numbers are wrong, do not buy the house. Period.

Shannon:
But what if you really, really, really want it?

Paul:
If you really, really, really want it and the numbers don't match?

Shannon:
Yeah.

Paul:

You need to walk away. There is no 'really want it.' You are not a non-profit organization, you have to be responsible to your business and your investors. You are in business to make money not to just make pretty houses.

Shannon:

Perfect. Pat, when you began your real estate investing career, how important was it for you to establish a team to help you be successful?

Patrick:

It was very important and that is why I liked the investment group I was in. We started out with a small team to help structure our business and properly file our taxes. We then added the realtors to help find and sell the properties and the contractors to repair the property. Both Paul and I worked full time at the beginning so we had to depend on contractors for almost everything. Our projects are generally light rehabs meaning the time from purchase to for sale was between four and six weeks. Our contractors consisted of the painter, plumber, electrician, roofer, and handyman. The real estate group was a great resource for getting referral for these contractors and others as we needed them. We then added more contractors as we needed them. I probably now have over 50 contractors in my phone. Everything from painters and drywall workers to foundation repair and concrete companies. We started with the core of contractors and added as we needed them.

Paul:

Yeah. I'm going to jump in here a little bit. I started doing the fix-and-flips right away. Pat was driving each day to work in Indiana, a long distance away. I started building the team.

We started with the core team of our real estate advisor's contractors. He had been a contractor for years and had many contacts. I was able to bounce ideas off of them because I was doing the fix-and-flips, and I needed to learn from the contractors so I could eliminate costly mistakes and rework. I had to learn how to get the right contractors in place at the right time. I had to make sure they had what they needed. I found that contractors like to talk and will tell you everything they know. I listened to each one of them about how they did their work and which contractors I could schedule together and which ones I could not. I learned a lot about secrets behind how to sequence the work. I was able to talk to some of these people that had experience doing the fix-and-flips, and doing the work, and actually get some great ideas on how to take care of special issues, how to measure a painter as to how well he does, that kind of stuff, and also how to get the project set up so that things run smoother for my team of painters and plumbers and electricians and to get the right people in at the right time.

Our real estate advisor let us use his teams to help build our team. His contractors also helped educate us on what to look for in contractors and how to tell a professional from an amateur.

Shannon:

Thank you. So do you feel like if you hadn't had that team, and if it would have just been you and Pat going at it alone, you would have been just as successful?

Paul:

Yes and no. Pat and I were dedicated to making this work but we knew we did not have the time or skills to do the work ourselves. If we did not have our advisor's contractors we probably would have spent more time looking at referral from friends, family, and co-workers. I would have had to learn through interviews. I have done that where I did not have a contractor so I asked multiple contractors to bid on a job. I made sure I was there and would ask them questions. They would tell me about the work that needed to be done and why. This was very educational and profitable. I mean, one of the major breaks that we got on the first two houses was information that I got from one of the team members. There was mold in a finished basement. I thought I had to tear it out, do mold remediation, and then re-finish the basement. The contractor suggested to just tear it out and do the mold remediation and not to refinish the basement. The house sold quickly even though the basement was unfinished. This suggestion saved us thousands of dollars on that project.

What advice will you give someone who is allowing fear to hold them back?

Patrick:
Actually, I think there are probably two things that will help people who are fearful about starting in real estate. One is to get a mentor. Someone they trust and someone who has already done what they want to do. They should have at least somebody they trust who they can ask questions when they get stuck.

The second is to put together a plan. Something they can follow. This is not a shoot-from-the-hip business. They actually have to put something together, a project plan. There is a way to do a house, a specific order.

But before they do their first house they must first create their business plan like we talked earlier. They must know what type of business fits them best and whether they want to do fix-and-flip, buy-and-hold, tax deeds, seller financed notes, multi-units or some other real estate business. They must define their business. The best part is that it's not carved in stone. If something is not working the business plan can be changed.

I've been in this business now for—what—eight years, and I'm still listening to the tapes and educational recordings. The one I was listening to today, says, "If you don't make an offer, you'll never get the house." You've got to go ahead and actually do it.

Shannon:
That's great advice.

Paul:
Yeah. I agree there. I mean, if you're just afraid of the unknown, if you don't have a plan, so you don't know what you're going to do, you don't know what you're going to run into, of course you're going to be afraid. So you create a plan, the plan takes most of the fear out of getting started. So all you really need is a plan and then stick to it.

Shannon:
What about multi-family dwellings?

Patrick:

We actually own three. We have a 15-unit building then we have a 3-unit and a 4-unit. So we do have some.

Shannon:

So if somebody wanted investment advice on multi-family dwellings, what would be three major things that they would need to know?

Patrick:

I think the first major thing an investor must know about multi-family units is to not manage them yourself. When we bought the 15-unit I tried to manage it for about 3 months. I have been managing the 4-unit for a few years, so the 15 unit should be fine. First problem is that the unit is 45 minutes from my house. Second, I began to feel like a Dad with a whole bunch of children. Calls at night "Someone's parked in my space," "so and so is playing their music too loud," "so and so yelled at me." What a mess. Save your sanity and hire a property manager. It's worth it.

Second, verify. If they don't give you accurate tax records showing rent rolls, expenses, etc. and additional income it's not true. Be sure to check the leases to verify the expected rent with the actual reported rent collected. If it's not on the tax records or they won't show it to you it doesn't exist.

Third, don't fall for the saying that their rents are below market rate and you can increase the rents after you buy the building. This is a great way to increase your vacancy rate. If they could have gotten a high rent, they would have because increased rents would increase the net operating income and increase the value of the building. Besides if you increase the rent as soon as you get the building the current tenants are more likely to move out. Great way to increase your vacancy rate, lower your net operating income, and the value of the building. Also don't fall for weird rental income such as AC rentals or charges, small heater rentals or charges, storage unit (especially if they are small) rentals unless the owner can show the charges being paid for years.

Shannon:

In a multi-family dwelling, what is different in the numbers than possibly with a single-family dwelling?

Patrick:

I built a spreadsheet and it'll go through and calculate the value of a rental building based on the gross income, net operating income. The spreadsheet calculates the cap rate, the cash on cash return, the expected monthly and yearly cash flow, the depreciation, and the actual value of the rental.

Paul:

Don't forget our buddy, taxes.

Patrick:

Yeah.

Shannon:

So what type of legacy do you want to leave?

Patrick:

I guess my biggest legacy that I'd like to leave is that I'm taking care of my family.

My mother lived 25 years longer than my father did. I want my wife to have the comforts that she deserves with retirement, as well as just taking care of her, making sure that she's properly taken care of even after I'm gone. So my biggest legacy is I want to leave her financially secure for her entire life.

For my children, I want them to have the ability to decide whether they want to work, follow their dreams, or do something else. They will eventually get these properties which will give them the ability to make their own choices as to what they want to do.

My daughter is a teacher who recently got married. These properties could, in the future, give her the option to stay home with the children or use the money to pay for college. They will have the freedom to decide.

My eldest son is an Information Systems Engineer and is doing very well but who knows whether someday he may want to start his own company. This could give him the financial security to go out on his own.

My youngest son is studying to be a pastor. His future is filled with opportunities. I want him to do what God has put in his heart to do.

I love my wife and children. Everything I do is for them. I want my legacy to be love. I did this for my family, my children's families, and their children's families.

Finally, I am the sixth and Paul is the seventh child of eight in a family that sometimes went to the Salvation Army to make ends meet. We built what many told us was impossible. We are proof that with determination, education, and support there are no restrictions on what a person can accomplish. You are your only restriction.

Paul:
Part of my legacy is to take care of my wife, make sure that she's always taken care of after I'm gone. She thinks I'm going first, so I'm guessing she'll need some help.

Both of my daughters have gone the serious Christian route. My youngest daughter married a youth minister. And my eldest daughter's husband does disaster recovery with Convoy of Hope. As both my daughter and my son-in-law are really interested in doing a Convoy of Hope disaster recovery type of work full time, I'd like to see them doing that. Fulfilling their dreams of what they really want to do with their lives and not have to worry about a nine-to-five or how they're going to get our next meal kind of thing.

And I also want them to remember me as generous and fun. I'm a fun dad who loves to spoil my children and grandchildren with love. For me the ultimate love you can leave behind is for your children to see your true love and sacrifice so they can have a wonderful and meaningful life.

Patrick:
God has blessed us both with more than we deserve. Everything we have is a gift from God.

Dr. Chau Ong

Dr. Chau Ong, Entrepreneur, Investor, Doctor of Pharmacy, Educator, Mentor, Dreamer & Freedom Enthusiast.

Dr. Chau Ong is passionate about helping people to be Healthy, Wealthy, and Happy! He has had many successes in many different fields such as medical, business, real estate, etc.

He started as an immigrant from Vietnam with nothing and had to share one bed in a tiny apartment room with his mom, dad, and sister for the first couple of years in the U.S.

Dr. Chau Ong vowed to take care of his family and leave a legacy for others by making a long lasting difference in each individual life that he has a chance to touch. He is very happy and grateful that he was able to buy a dream home for his parents and grandma and is taking care of their retirement.

Dr. Chau Ong has created a unique system that really revolutionizes the real estate industry by increasing cash flow from rentals by 500-700 percent. He has done this by advancing his investing strategies to corporate and vacation rentals. He is happy to help many others to do the same and achieve financial freedom 5-7 times faster! Dr. Chau Ong is also working on projects that integrate healthcare, entrepreneurship, and real estate. These include, but are not limited to, assisted living, nursing homes, medical offices, medical buildings, etc.

He believes that each individual has unlimited untapped potential, and we can have our wildest dreams come true if we are persistent and consistent at tapping into our potential. We truly can have it all! His lifetime dream & mission is to impact a billion lives by tapping into their potential and creating long lasting change in the world in the areas of health, wealth, and happiness.

Dr. Chau Ong loves traveling, hiking, dancing, serving the church & the community, new adventures & experiences, and most importantly, connecting with dreamers!

Contact Info:
www.chauong.com
www.buyorsellyourhousefast.com
email: intlprosperity@gmail.com

Shannon:
Dr. Ong what inspired you to get into real estate?

Dr. Chau Ong:
Real estate is what I found the best tool for creating wealth and financial freedom, not just for you but your family, and to leave a legacy as well. I've been involved in many, many kind of businesses and have a Bachelor in Business and took many MBA classes. I have not yet to find a better business to create residual, long-term, passive income by leveraging other people's money, energy, and time. If you do it right, it can be recession proof. It does not matter what your profession is, everybody should invest in real estate, at least passively. Everybody should have some real estate to create that passive income in order to gain true freedom and security for you and your family!

Shannon:
So you said that 'no matter what your profession is'... so do you feel like everyone should be full-time real estate investors? Or do you feel like it's OK to be both the pharmacist and a real estate investor? Or are you going to eventually stop doing pharmaceutical work?

Dr. Chau Ong:
Sure. So it's different for everybody, right? Doing it full-time or not is up to you, whether you really love the profession or not. Some people, they don't. If it's not their thing, it's fine. Even if it's not your passion, wouldn't it be awesome to leverage other people's skills and time to achieve financial freedom through passive income from real estate? There are many real estate investors who would love to partner with someone who has the money but no time or no passion in real estate. It's a win win situation for both!

For example, I'm working on 11-unit luxury riverfront townhomes that I will convert to vacation and corporate rentals. The cash flow on it after expenses and mortgage will be $16,000/month. It is such an amazing cash flow that I can offer 15 percent return per year for passive investors! How would you like to be earning 15 percent return back by real estate and do zero work?!

Another option is equity partnership. I'm raising $500,000 for 50 percent equity of this deal. That would mean the investor(s) will earn $8,000/month cash flow, another $8,000/month through 10 percent appreciation of that market, another $8,000/month in amortization and depreciation tax benefits. Isn't it awesome that you can increase your net worth by about $32,000/month without doing any work for it?

So it doesn't matter what your profession is in order to have financial, residual passive income, real estate is the answer. If you want the best tools to leverage against inflation, against the market, against all of the economy and everything like that, then real estate is, definitely, one of the best tools, if not the best tool for that.

As far as for myself, I want to integrate healthcare and real estate together. I'm working on projects that are in the realm of medical building, assisted living, etc. Basically, utilizing my knowledge & background to work in the healthcare field and integrate real estate and healthcare together.

Shannon:

That's awesome. So you have actually commented two or three times on passive income and creating passive income. What exactly is passive income? And why is it so important?

Dr. Chau Ong:

Passive income is, basically, residual income. That's money coming in whether you work or not. The main goal of any entrepreneur is to remove yourself from your business and have it still going. That's the ultimate dream. That is really, truly, a business owner. A lot of people will say they own a business but they're actually own a job. If they take themselves away from their business, their business shuts down within three to six months. But with real estate, you can receive tremendous interest on your money, have someone manage it, and you enjoy your dream lifestyle!

So passive income is where the check's coming in whether you work or not. And it's residual income so that way you can really live the lifestyle that you want to live.

Shannon:

Perfect. So how did you figure out your niche was vacation & corporate rentals? Or did you kind of just fall into it?

Dr. Chau Ong:

Yeah, so it took me awhile, right? I started out like most real estate investors, just doing regular rentals like everybody else. And then one time I took my family to vacation in Hawaii. We booked this $7 million mansion overlooking the whole island. It's gorgeous, and it's like $4,000 a week. So I was like, "Whoa—there's something going on here, $4,000/week!" It was worth it! So I started looking into it and I happened to live in a beach city. So I was like, "Yeah. Why not give it a shot. I think it will work. The numbers will look good." So we did it. The first year we set everything up and then the second year is when it really started flowing. And then we expanded our businesses; now we rent out to executives and managers from companies who they don't really care too much about the cost.

Shannon:

Awesome. Now this is on a Texas coastline?

Dr. Chau Ong:

No. This is actually in Charleston, South Carolina, and I live in Texas.

Shannon:

South Carolina? Okay.

Dr. Chau Ong:

Yeah, and I have my vacation rental and corporate rental over there in South Carolina on the coast. We have teams and systems in place that I didn't even need to fly out there at all for the past year!

Shannon:

What made you decide to go to South Carolina. You said you were living there at the time?

Dr. Chau Ong:

Yeah. I actually was living in South Carolina. I moved to Texas two years ago because family and the market out here is really good, too, but yeah, mostly for family.

Shannon:

Perfect. Okay. Tell me some ways when you are looking to acquire a property. What is a creative way that you have used to acquire a property?

Dr. Chau Ong:

Absolutely, so a creative way would be using other people›s money, using other people›s leverage and time in order to get into the property. I was able to raise some money from my personal contacts and able to get into those deals, and then we just share the ownership, the cash flow, and the future resale value of the house.

Shannon:

All right. You just touched on using other people's money and resources. That sounds really easy, other than I've never been able to walk up to someone and say, "You want to give me a couple of hundred thousand dollars so I can buy a house?" What do you mean by that? How do you use other people's money and resources?

Dr. Chau Ong:

You can always start out with what's in it for them, right? I always start with what kind of value I can add to other people's money. It's not about what you want. It's about what you can provide to other people because people don't care about what we want, what you or I want, they care about themselves, right?

Shannon:

Right.

Dr. Chau Ong:

So you can show people what's in it for them first. What do they want? How'd they get there? After all of that, most people will want more money and more time. Just show them how real estate can help them do that because real estate is the best thing to gain more money and gain more time. You've just got to show them the value in it, how it would appreciate over time. Real estate, historically, has been increasing over time. Hedging against inflation and with a cash flow in a business, real estate is really amazing!

You only need about 20 to 30 percent down into a house, so let's say you buy a house and use somebody else's money for the 20 percent down and then that house appreciate, in my market, 10 percent a year. In two years, you've made 100 percent of the money back. That's 100 percent return in two years just on the appreciation.

Shannon:

Right.

Dr. Chau Ong:

Now on the cash flow, for example, on a $100,000 house I put $20,000 down. Well, using our advanced strategies of vacation and corporate rental, we are cash flowing at $1,000-$2,000/month per house right now. I'm going to be conservative and say $1000 a month. We are able to generate $12,000 a year, so you take $12,000/$20,000 down payment, that's about 60 percent return!. Within two years, I get my money back and then make 60 percent return on my money! You see what I'm saying? Within those two strategies, these two things right there, you're looking at like a 220 percent return on my money within only two years, and then you can also have a tax write off strategy, amortization strategy, which means that the tenants are paying your mortgage so over time the mortgage will go down. The cash flow will go up so you have more equity in the house so it's just amazing! The stock market at its best years would be 10-15 percent a year, consistently.

Shannon:

Yeah. I don't know many other places you can invest like that and make that kind of money.

Dr. Chau Ong:
Right.

Shannon:
You're telling me about all these things and for someone who's not a real estate investor that sounds a little overwhelming. I don't know how to calculate tax write offs and amortization and how to make sure that I got the right cash flow. When you began your real estate investing career, did you just know all this or did you have help from other people?

Dr. Chau Ong:
Oh, yeah, totally. I just went in and knew everything, and I did everything right from day one, and it was awesome!

Shannon:
Perfect.

Dr. Chau Ong:
[Laugh] Just kidding! Everything is through trial and error, right?

Shannon:
Right.

Dr. Chau Ong:
Just like any profession, you got to get the right education, the right mentor. You know what really amazed me is that people would spend hundreds of thousands of dollars on college and never blink an eye, but then when they look at investing in themselves getting a coach or mentor for real estate they think it's different. People spend a hundred to two hundred grand on a college degree to learn all the craft and go through years and years of schooling in order to make $50,000 to $120,000/year, and they wouldn›t spend 10 to 20 grand on their own education in real estate and being mentored by multi-millionaires to make multiple six & seven figures income? It doesn't really make sense, does it?

Shannon:
No. It doesn't.

Dr. Chau Ong:
Right. Every profession you need education, right?

Shannon:
Yes.

Dr. Chau Ong:
In every profession, you need a mentor, right?

Shannon:
Right.

Dr. Chau Ong:
There's no difference in real estate. You do need to get the right education so I went to every guru seminar that I could find. I read everything I could put my hands on, watched all the videos, all that stuff in the beginning so I spent tens of thousands of dollars going to these things, flying all over the U.S. trying to find the right mentor. All of that was good, but what we have right now with our company is the best. The community that we are able to be a part of right now is the best community and the best education I have ever found.

Shannon:
Have you ever called one of your mentors and said, "Hey, I've got this great deal. It's awesome," and they looked at it and said either, "Oh my gosh. Yes it is and this is why," or, "Ooh, no it's not, and this is"?

Dr. Chau Ong:
Oh, yes. Yes. I did and, yeah, he basically pointed out, "Oh, hey. You didn't see this." "Hey, you looked at the million potential process, but you didn't see that it's in a war zone." You know?

Shannon:

Right.

Dr. Chau Ong:

Or, "Is there is reason why they're selling it"? It's an underperforming asset. They have thousands of units, but why are they selling this 100-unit? Because it's underperforming and it's in a war zone, in a bad neighborhood.

Shannon:

Right.

Dr. Chau Ong:

Number one, you don't want to buy in the war zone. There are some rules that you definitely need to go by in order to maximize results for the best practices of real estate or any industry.

Shannon:

Tell me. What are your best practices? When you're looking for a property, tell me the top three things that you look for?

Dr. Chau Ong:

Cash flow is number one. Job growth/appreciation number two. The property condition number three. We also need an Avatar for the deal, which includes your target buyer, market and the property.

Shannon:

Are you a fix and flip or a buy and hold investor?

Dr. Chau Ong:

If there is a fix and flip that comes my way, yeah, sure, I'll do it, but ultimately, your end goal is have a lot of rentals. That way you can really achieve financial freedom.

Shannon:

Right.

Dr. Chau Ong:

Fix and flip is sexy on TV. It's sexy. It looks good but, at the end of the day, you got to do it all over again.

Shannon:

At the end of the day, 20 years from now that's not so sexy just like people.

Dr. Chau Ong:

Yeah, exactly. You know what? Twenty years from now, my rental is going to be paid off and that's pretty sexy because it's $3,000/month cash flow per house! Ten of them will be $30,000/month! My goal is to own 100 of them, that's $300,000/month! Then own 1000 of them, that's $3,000,000/month!

Shannon:

You may not be sexy anymore, but that rental still will be.

Dr. Chau Ong:

Yeah, exactly!

Shannon:

Tell me the top three best practices. What are the top three things that you look for?

Dr. Chau Ong:

Of the top three things, number one is the numbers. Yeah. I don't even look at a property first before I look at the numbers because the numbers are what matter. The numbers don't lie. People do. Your thoughts do. Your emotions do, but the numbers don't lie. They're going to tell you the truth. If the numbers don't make sense, then there's no sense of driving out there, looking at it, or whatever. It doesn't matter what it looks like.

Shannon:

Okay.

Dr. Chau Ong:

And then it's what the property looks like. I buy pretty houses at a discount so I buy houses that are built in the 2000s. If it's built in the 2000s, 90 percent of the time there's not much going on with it to fix, so I can sleep like a baby at night and I don't have to worry about people calling me or fixing things, and blah, blah, blah.

Great potential cash flow location is very important, as always, but again, it's all about the numbers, the cash flow.

Shannon:

Okay. You've been investing in real estate for quite a while; however, you have only been with the community you've been with for a short amount of time. How has your education in real estate changed the way that you invest?

Dr. Chau Ong:

Yes, absolutely. It's more advanced! With the community I'm part of right now, I learned a lot of the techniques I know. It's enabled me to triple, quadruple my cash flow. Number two, the tax strategies are so advanced that it blew my mind because I never learned about any of that from the other groups that I paid more for.

Valerie M. Sargent

This expert knows how to bring vitality to individuals and organizations! Valerie M. Sargent has spent her career within the multifamily industry, with a focus on the property management aspects of the business. As an entrepreneur and President of Yvette Poole & Associates, she is a highly sought after national speaker, trainer and consultant within the multifamily industry and beyond. Her specialties include leasing, sales, marketing, customer service, leadership and emotional intelligence. In 2013, Valerie pursued a Level 1 & Level 2 TalentSmart Emotional Intelligence (EQ) certification after seeing a need to help all company employees enhance their self-understanding, teamwork, and communication. She is passionate about helping people increase their EQ through her "It's in the Pause"® training sessions, TalentSmart classes, and EQ Executive Coaching.

Valerie is a daughter, sister, and proud aunt to her wonderful nieces and nephews! Growing up landlocked in the Midwest, she fell in love at first visit with Southern California, where she has now lived longer than any other state. She cherishes friendship, connection, and contribution and loves to give back to causes and communities that are important to her.

Contact Info:
www.valeriemsargent.com • www.ypooleandassoc.com.

Shannon:

What inspired you to get into real estate? Did you move to Orange County to get into real estate?

Valerie:

No, I moved to Orange County because I was landlocked growing up in Kansas and Oklahoma, and I fell in love with the ocean and cooler temperatures!

I suppose, in a way, I've always been involved with real estate. As a young girl, my mom was a real estate agent. I remember her driving around Wichita, Kansas, with signs in the trunk of her car. On nights she had an open house, my dad—who was an attorney—was extremely proud of the TV dinners he made for us. Ha! He brought his 'A game' to the kitchen for sure.

After that, my mom went into the multifamily industry on the property management side. She managed apartment communities and eventually did some marketing as well. I was about 12 years old when I first started in the business, helping her hang newsletters on apartment community doors.

My multifamily career *formally* started between college semesters in Oklahoma. Upon Mom's return from an out-of-town marketing assignment, she found that her boss—a family friend—had hired me as a leasing consultant for the summer. It was my first onsite experience, and I loved it! I leased for two different summers when home from college. My older brother was in the mortgage industry at that time, and he became a mortgage banker. See? All in the family!

I went into the multifamily industry full-time after college graduation—first as a leasing consultant and then as an assistant manager. I never wanted to be a manager. Instead, I took the path toward marketing and training. As Regional Marketing Director for a company that transitioned from a private entity to a publicly traded REIT, I had marketing and training responsibilities for 7 properties in Oklahoma and 15 in Dallas prior to my move.

I relocated to California in 1998 and worked for a privately owned and operated property management company. I was happy to be back with a private company, and I conducted marketing and training efforts within their ancillary services and utility billing divisions. I was exposed to opportunities for multifamily owners to increase their net operating income through additional sources of revenue besides just rental payments, through things like utility cost recovery, telecommunications, furniture rental, laundry facilities, and more.

When I left that company in 2005, I partnered in business with my former boss and dear friend, Yvette. I continued my love of training and really developed my passion for speaking, training, and consulting within the multifamily industry and beyond. I now conduct training for property management companies and speak at several company and apartment association events across the nation, including the National Apartment Association Education Conference.

Being an educator within the multifamily field of real estate by trade is part of what got me interested in real estate, as the multifamily industry opened my eyes to what's possible with real estate investing. I've watched it all in action for years.

Shannon:

That's awesome. So, you've always been in real estate. It sounds like you've done several things, and your family has done several things. I'm guessing that when you said to your mom, "Hey Mom, I think I'm going to take this to the next level and start investing in real estate," that she was very supportive of that?

Valerie:

Absolutely. My mom is one of my biggest cheerleaders and biggest fans, and she is certainly also one of my best friends. I'm very lucky. When I told her I had the opportunity to learn more about investing, it made sense to her. We've both seen things from the property management side, watching so many owners be successful in this business. We also both realize how much it takes to get into real estate investing and how it can help create different futures for people.

Shannon:

When you were getting into your real estate investing career and you decided to add the investing side to your portfolio, did you think you were going to stay in multifamily, or were you going to focus on different strategies, such as fix and flip or 'subject to' lease options?

Valerie:
Multifamily is really interesting right now. After the crash, Morgan Stanley said we've become a renter nation. This has been the first time we've seen renting outpace the American dream of home ownership, and it's been a remarkable time for real estate investors and the property management industry. It's never happened before.

With people in situations with distressed homes for sale, foreclosures, lower prices on the market, and credit issues, investors started buying single family homes and turning them into rentals as those home prices were rising again. Multifamily communities traded hands and new construction started exploding to handle the rental growth, the downsizing of Baby Boomers and new Millennial renters coming into the rental housing market. It's been an opportune time to be an investor.

Having said that, I'm open to whatever deals make sense overall for my financial goals. So if the right situation crosses my path, who knows?

I love the transformative process and the faster return on investment for the short term when you do something like a fix and flip. It was my own accidental fix and flip that truly allowed me to see the power of real estate investing, when I saw how real estate changed my life personally.

From that point I began to think, "Okay. That was an accident. How do I do that strategically instead of accidentally?" I knew I needed to learn. I had a friend who said, "You know all of the executives at these companies. Why don't you have them teach you?"

I realized large multifamily owners weren't going to take me by the hand and teach me everything they knew. Nobody has time for that. I knew I needed to invest in myself first and become educated so I could learn to strategically invest in real estate in order to build a better future and retirement for myself.

I'm looking at buying and holding single and multifamily real estate as part of my longer-range goals, hopefully with friends and other industry partners I care about. It all depends on what opportunities are available. You never know what's going to come across your path. I simply look for opportunities and am open to different situations.

Shannon:

All right. Let's go back and touch on multifamily. If someone came to you and said, "Hey, I really want to invest in multifamily dwellings," what's one of the most important things they need to know?

Valerie:

I'll come at this from a bit of a different angle that I don't think people new to multifamily investing automatically think about, since they're more focused on write-offs and cash flow. If they're going to be successful with multifamily investing, equally as important—or perhaps more so—is management.

You'll likely hire a third-party management company if you don't end up managing the units yourself, especially with larger communities. I've seen owners not put enough consideration into recommended budgeting, and they try to cut corners. My first advice would be to ensure that some type of budget for education is available. This can be through local apartment associations, online resources, or in-person training sessions and classes.

I say this because leasing apartments is a skill that must be developed. Your front office team members are crucial to your success. Their training will help keep your buildings full. As an owner, you may not realize that you, along with the team members themselves, are at risk of being sued for Fair Housing implications when you have staff who are not properly trained out on the front line and they mistakenly (or purposefully) violate local or federal fair housing laws.

It's sad that this still has to be a concern today, but the Fair Housing Act is federal law that helps prevent discrimination against the seven protected classes, which are race, color, national origin, religion, sex, familial status, and disability. In fact, anyone who owns more than three single-family homes as rentals would be subject to this law as a landlord.

Beyond federal law, there are sometimes local, city, or state mandates that provide additional protection for classes such as sexual orientation, marital status, and others. If they've never had any experience with rentals, people may not grasp what's involved or expected of them in that regard when they're just getting started. This is why it's helpful to engage a skilled property management company familiar with all multifamily requirements.

Proper training ensures your leasing team is capable and competent, allowing you to be confident they can handle leasing responsibilities professionally. Realize that money budgeted for training is money well spent in keeping your apartment units occupied and reducing your overall exposure for risk.

Another bit of advice: Don't micro-manage the property management company you hire to handle your community. It is incredibly important to be involved in what's happening with your assets. Yet as a multifamily consultant, I can't tell you how many property management executives I have known or worked with as clients through the years who have had fee management owners occupying way too much of their time with unrealistic demands and micro-management. You hired them to do a job. Let them do it, and then establish times to review their performance. Calling and emailing them at all hours and expecting things that are not being asked for from their other clients will not help them be more effective for you. Letting them do the work you hired them to do will allow for that.

Lastly, be prepared to maintain your asset. Have proper money budgeted for ongoing maintenance supplies, necessary projects, and capital expenditures. Your property managers will work diligently to stay within your budget, but being constrained with scarcely budgeted dollars available for these necessary expenses will lead to poor customer service, challenging vendor relationships, decreased resident retention, and increased turnover.

Shannon:
You touched on how important it is to have the units leased. Wouldn't you think that one of the advantages to having a multifamily dwelling is that it's really just not that big of a deal if you have two or three empty units because you have cash flow coming from the other units, right?

Valerie:

This depends on how many units you have overall. If you have a multi-family building that's only 28 units and 4 people all move out at the same time, you could have 4 empty units—a 14 percent vacancy rate. You're not going to have enough cash flow if you can't get them leased right away. But if you had a larger community of 500 units, that's a workable percentage. Five apartments there is only a 1 percent loss to vacancy. Much more manageable.

This goes back to having competent staff handling marketing, phone calls, and emails with prospects, and effectively selling the apartments. As the market has started rounding out again, companies have said to me, "Our onsite teams haven't had to work for leases in recent years, but we think we need help brushing up on their leasing skills. Leasing consultants got used to prospects just walking in the door and renting."

When the market turns, marketing and training become more important, yet it's sometimes a budget item that gets cut. Don't do this.

Shannon:

What is a realistic expectation for an investor to have as a percentage for empty units?

Valerie:

Well, obviously, 100 percent occupancy is the goal, but in multifamily the amount of resident turnover usually averages around 40 percent annually. It isn't possible to get 100 percent all the time. I see many companies target 95 percent occupancy or above as a goal. Anytime you get down in the 80s, it's a concern. Obviously lower numbers mean lower cash flow to run the properties and generate profit.

There are regular, ongoing expenses from an operational aspect to think about: landscaping needs, office expenses, unit turns, regular maintenance including tools and supplies... all of the things that go into owning a building. If you don't have enough rent coming in to meet your budgetary requirements, positive cash flow will be difficult.

Shannon:

When you're talking to an investor who is transitioning into having a leasing team or property management company, what would be your goal? If 95 percent is the goal at all times, would you tell the property manager or investor to shoot for 90 percent for it to be effective? Or 95 percent? When they ask, "What can I budget for? Where's my fudge room?" what would be a realistic goal?

Valerie:

It depends on the owner/investor, what numbers they need, and how much flexibility they have. It's also based on the total number of units, as discussed earlier. A smaller number of units demands a higher occupancy percentage.

If you hire a property management company, they usually have budgeting and goals set regarding occupancy percentages as part of their service to the owner. It will be something for the owner to discuss and decide with the company based on their financial objectives and desired NOI.

You have a physical occupancy percentage, and you have a leased percentage. Sometimes you may have a lower occupancy percentage than desired based on timing of move-outs, but all the apartments coming available may already be leased. When you receive a notice-to-vacate, you have an opportunity to pre-lease that apartment. In that scenario, you have covered your rental in advance.

You will want to budget for a loss to vacancy covering the time to turn a unit and get it ready for the next renter. You're not budgeting to have apartments sitting vacant for months at a time. The goal is to lease that apartment in advance or shortly after it becomes available for move-in, so you don't have much downtime. I target ten days vacant, five to turn, and five to lease in a strong market.

I've been hired by owners/management companies to assess troubled apartment communities for possible issues—for instance, why an occupancy rate is hovering in the 70s. I look to see if they are priced correctly for the market. If apartments are vacant a long time, I sometimes find they are sticking to rental rates that are too high. That loss to vacancy can be far more damaging than if they had lowered the rental rate to be more in line with the surrounding area.

Let's face it—prices are high in Southern California! Yet I've seen apartment rents be $200-$900 higher than area competitors. Although an apartment's quality may be higher than others nearby, you also have to consider what the market will allow and be realistic. Keep this in mind for upgrades, too.

If you had an apartment sit vacant for three months priced at $2,500 when the market average is $1,900, you're looking at a loss to vacancy of $7,500 over that 3-month period. If you'd rented the apartment for $2,100, the apartment would be occupied and that $400/month you're missing totals $4,800 for the year. That's $2,700 less than what you lost over the three months it stood vacant due to unrealistic pricing. Don't be stubborn. Know what the market will stand, and plan accordingly. Look into yield management.

Shannon:

When you begin your real estate investing career, how important is it to establish a team to help you be successful?

Valerie:

Teams are very important. They will differ based on the investing strategies you use. For instance, vendor relationships are very important in multifamily. I have the ability to pick up the phone and call several different individuals when I have specific questions or need a particular type of work done, thanks to my amazing network. For my investing, I also have coaching I can receive in either a group or a one-on-one basis. Any time I need additional guidance, I know have the relationships and teams necessary to help me avoid potential pitfalls.

Shannon:

That's awesome. So many people try and go at it on their own. Do you feel like when people who do that, it's one of the main reasons they fail in real estate investing?

Valerie:

There could be many reasons why people fail in real estate investing. Hopefully we don't "fail," but we learn important lessons. Although some lessons can be very expensive, right?! I think some people try to do deals too soon before they know exactly what to do. They may go into a situation feeling over-confident with a little knowledge. Others may over-leverage themselves. Some people don't have a contingency plan in place. If anything goes sideways, they don't know where to go from there. I've seen people who don't run numbers properly for a deal to ensure it actually works, especially in the case of unexpected repairs or situations. If they don't work this into their numbers, they get into trouble. These are some things that could prevent real estate investing success, in addition to not having resources, a network, or a community you connect with (who may have made the mistakes you want to avoid) who can help advise you along the way.

Shannon:

If someone was going to get started in real estate investing, and they had very little money and possibly poor credit, but really wanted to get started, what would you recommend they do first?

Valerie:

Aside from having quality real estate investing education as part of their investing foundation, relationships and a network are extremely important. Realize that it's possible to do deals using what we like to call OPM—Other People's Money. Or even OPC—Other People's Credit.

Shannon:

Okay.

Valerie:

Having productive, one-on-one conversations with people to let them know they can get double digit returns on their self-directed IRAs through investing in real estate can provide funds necessary for a deal. Raising private money is a great way for people to raise money for real estate. Many people don't realize they can self-direct their retirement accounts, or they may be looking for investment opportunities. You'll only find out if you're willing to have conversations about money and you let people know what you're doing.

Most people don't like to talk about money. We've always been taught that it's something we shouldn't discuss. But if you're going to be an investor, you have to be willing to talk about money.

Shannon:

Where do you find people? It's not as easy as just walking up and you make small talk and people say, "Oh, what do you do?" and you respond, "Well, I'm a real estate investor. Do you have any money?"

Valerie:

Ha! That's like if you see someone across a room and decide you want to date them and just walk up to them before having a conversation and say, "You're awesome. Can I call you?" You don't necessarily want to put the cart before the horse. You can finesse the conversation toward the results you want.

Shannon:

How do you do that? You're at dinner, you're at your kid's soccer game, you're wherever and you see that they have a nice handbag and you think, "I wonder what they do for a living?" How do you approach that, "Would you like to be an investor?"

Valerie:

I often start with, "How are you?" I introduce myself. Don't be afraid of small talk. People will often ask, "What do you do?" Have a prepared answer and let everyone know what you're doing. So, an example for someone doing flips might be, "I'm a real estate investor, and I partner with people to help them get better returns on their retirement accounts so they can maximize their investments, too. I focus mainly on fix and flips. In fact, I just found a great deal under market for $140,000. After repairs and expenses, I'm looking to net a profit of around $25,000. I love what I do! Have you ever thought about real estate investing as part of your retirement plan, or do you know someone wanting to get into that?"

Be natural and authentic. People are attracted to what you're doing. When I say have conversations, many times it's with people in your life currently. Be able to talk to everyone and feel comfortable discussing what you're doing.

Shannon:

Does that scare you at all? How many friends have you had that say, "Hey, I've got Pampered Chef, I've got Thirty-One, I've got Amway, I've got Tupperware." What do you say to the people who are afraid to talk to their network already? What advice could you give someone who is really just kind of allowing fear to keep them from having those conversations?

Valerie:

Fear is a scary thing isn't it? People get caught in fear for many different reasons, whether it's fear of having conversations or fear of getting into investing. I would first ask those people, "What is behind your fear? Where is that fear coming from?" I encourage them to deal with those answers first. Then they can develop goals, a time-line, a plan, and conversations.

This is where a community is valuable because they teach you how to have those conversations. Education teaches you how to have those conversations. Many people know it's important to have multiple income streams, and there are a lot of people who have tried—some with successful results, and some... not so much.

I think people who are open to real estate investing are open to entrepreneurial experiences and may have tried some of those things before. I had. If you find just one person interested in what you're doing, it becomes a template for attracting other interested parties. The difference is that real estate is an investment and a secured asset with greater potential for profit, instead of products being sold.

Shannon:

As you're touching on education, you've done so much teaching in your life. Now you are not only being a teacher but also a student. How has your education in real estate changed the way you invest?

Valerie:

Probably one of the most important things I see in looking at what others have done that I know to do differently is watching people do real estate investing in their own name to create cash flow. I realize they're not structuring themselves properly in order to protect their finances and assets should anything happen. I've learned there should be separation between your personal life and your investing life, which involves setting up proper legal entities to do your real estate investing. That's more of a tax and legal investing strategy, but I think it's incredibly valuable. You want to make sure you protect yourself properly.

Some people learn just one real estate investing strategy. I'm interested in several because I know different strategies work at different times in the economy and the market. It's important to know how to change from one to the next in case there's a shift in what's happening.

Shannon:
Let's elaborate on that. In a strong economy, what is one of the investment strategies you would use to acquire a property? Also, on the flip side of that, in a weak housing economy, what is a property acquisition strategy you would want to use?

Valerie:
Well, I mentioned earlier that my first fix and flip was accidental. I acquired my first condo in Mission Viejo in 2002. I bought it for $207,500 at that time. Afterward, I could see housing market prices going up the rails like a roller coaster nearing the top of the hill. I sold it after two years for $335,000, slightly under market at the time to move it before things turned.

We must pay attention to what's going on with the economy and the market and realize that real estate is cyclical. When things are strong, people are trying to sell at the top of the market. If anything happens with the economy when a market is low, it's a good time for investors to buy. When the economy is struggling a bit, you may want to practice a buy and hold strategy rather than a flip in that scenario. Smart investors are able to do creative deals at a time when the economy is challenged, perhaps helping people.

I've watched the cyclical nature happen throughout my years in multifamily. It comes in waves. You can always depend that it will go up and it will come down. But, real estate is an incredibly solid investment over time. People always need housing.

Shannon:

So many people I speak to are scared by the numbers in Southern California. Since you have such a strong network, have you thought about going into other areas outside Southern California, or are you confident in that market and want to stay there?

Valerie:

Absolutely! It has been important to me to plug into other communities throughout not only California but across the U.S. as well. I interact with other markets from Seattle to Arkansas, from Chicago to DC. Last week when I was in Atlanta speaking at the NAA Conference, I was able to plug into our local community there and tour one of their potential fix and flips. When you see what's happening in other markets, you get ideas of what you might want to implement.

Because Southern California is so expensive, I can look at other markets where real estate may be more affordable and deals may be more prevalent. I have consciously built a network to connect with in other locations, and they already have teams in place who can assist me. Having a strong foundation of relationships is key to getting deals done.

Initially I was intimidated by the prices in Southern California, thinking I wanted to go out of state. Yet after meeting some of our local investors here, I realized they're doing the exact same thing, just at a higher level.

So it goes back to that fear. What are you afraid of? Yes, that's a bigger risk. But, if you know what you're doing and you do things effectively, it's just doing it at another level. I learned to see opportunities for a higher level of return, thanks to working with different investors who showed me what is possible in this market as well.

Shannon:

I know you have a ton of knowledge, which is actually great because so many people get started and they don't have all this knowledge.

Valerie:

Thank you. My years as a trainer and educator helped me realize that things we're taught in school don't necessarily prepare us to even buy a house. I remember sitting down with my friend Carrie and her husband Brian when I was going to buy that first condo. He told me, "You can do it." He actually gave me a spreadsheet to help work out the numbers and make me feel more comfortable with it. Even then, I had a mentor when buying for the first time.

Many people out there don't know what they're doing or where to turn, even with buying their own homes and investing in their own real estate. I knew how important it was for me to learn all of the different aspects because I'm such a believer in education. I knew I needed something accessible, with classes I could repeat at any time and learn over and over, being exposed to the same, updated information in different ways. It helps me retain information so when I employ those strategies in a deal, I can do them effectively. It's so important that you feel knowledgeable and comfortable in what you're doing, regardless of your investment strategy.

Shannon:
What is the legacy that you want to leave?

Valerie:

Ahh, that's a nice question.... My purpose in life is to make a difference and to ignite positive change in others. I love helping people find solutions to their most pressing needs. Whether I do this all through real estate investing, speaking, training, emotional intelligence, coaching, or consulting, or simply as a loving friend and family member, I hope I am perceived as an authentic, heart-centered lover of life and all of its beautiful gifts.

I want to help others lead lives of joy, abundance, and love, leading first by example. When I'm most attuned, I find that life embraces me with resonance, purpose, and grace... I recognize this.

I am feeling very emotional right now talking about this because I found out this week that I'm losing a friend to cancer. She has just gone home to be with her family during her final days. So, I find myself thinking of Katy and the legacy she is leaving behind right now. She is such a bright light and will be terribly missed. I dedicate this chapter to her and to my other friends lost to cancer too soon, including my best childhood friend, Jenny. I'd especially like to acknowledge my nephew, Steven, who was only 18 when he lost his battle to cancer. I am grateful that he taught us all about strength, bravery, perseverance, and family.

Circling back to my legacy, I suppose I would like to remind everyone that we must live and embrace this life we've been given at every possible moment. I lost my dad when I was only 14 years old, and I learned this lesson at a very young age. Life itself is the true gift. We never know how long we have—be sure to make the most of the present.

So that is something I wish to extend to others: A joy of living life and helping in whatever way I can to contribute to others living their lives more fully. Then, when my time here on Earth is through, I will be happy if my legacy is that of love, kindness, and laughter... but most especially, love.

Richard Stock

Richard Stock began his real estate business in 2005. He has over 14 years of experience in investing and running his own business. In 2012, he was recognized as the number one income earner for Renatus and has remained in the top three ever since.

Under Richard's leadership, his team, 212, has become one of the most successful groups in Renatus—earning many awards and creating the company's top leaders.

Richard graduated from Utah State University in 2001 with a Bachelor's degree in Finance and Marketing with a minor in Economics.

Richard and his wife Amy live in Sandy, Utah, with their three sons.

Shannon:

What inspired you to get into real estate?

Richard:

Years ago I had a good friend whom I respected, and I was talking to his mom one day while I was attending college. She asked me, "Richard, what are you going to do when you grow up? I know you aren't enjoying college. You're a hard worker, but you just aren't the type of person that can sit down at a desk for eight hours a day." I said, "I don't know, that's what I'm trying to figure out." She responded, "You know, Richard, I think you'd do really well doing two things: running your own business and investing in real estate." That's something that stuck with me for 16 years.

Two years later, I was talking to another friend's dad, who also had done well financially. I asked him, "If you were to do it all over again what would you do?" He said, "Richard, I'd do the same two things I'm doing now. I'd run my own business and I'd invest in real estate." As I learned from these individuals, who were financially free, I decided I too would get into real estate. I started on that journey, and I've been able to have a lot of success.

Shannon:

According to Forbes magazine, real estate is one of the top three ways people become wealthy. As a real estate expert, why do you feel this is the case?

Richard:

Real estate has been a great way for me to leverage my time. I take a small down payment and I buy a home. I can put renters into that home. They're going to work 160 hours a month if single, or 320 hours a month as a couple, to pay their most important bill of the month, which is going to be their rent. I then get the money, and I pay down the mortgage. Not only do I get what is left over as cash flow, I also get the appreciation. I can then write off the interest and depreciation on my taxes, and I'm able to create wealth every single month.

The other reason I love real estate is I'm able to leverage time and money. Years ago, when I had a W-2 job, I realized I could be sitting at my cubicle while other people were out working on a home. They would fix it up for me. They'd do paint, carpet, remodel the kitchen, the bathroom, whatever needed to be done. They would fix the home up make it really nice for me as I'm sitting in my cubicle. I'm following up and checking to make sure work is being done. At the end of the day, over a three or four-month period, I could work 30-40 hours and get a good massive check on each transaction. By using that massive income, I can get passive income.

Shannon:
If someone has very little money or poor credit, what are some strategies to get into real estate investing?

Richard:
Oh, man. That's a great question. That was exactly me. When I got into investing six and a half years ago, I was drowning in debt. I had a 580 credit score. I was negative $7,000 a month. I had no money and I had no credit.

However, I've learned that raising money is one of the easiest things to do. I've been able to do multiple real estate transactions without using my money or my credit. As I've been able to teach others how to do the same, it's been a huge blessing in my life and theirs. You can learn how to use other people's money to be able to be a successful investor.

Shannon:
In your business, how do you teach others about real estate?

Richard:
We have briefings where people learn about the Renatus educational system. Renatus is a place where individuals can be trained by 24 practitioners who have made millions of dollars in their respective fields. If people just implement and follow the proven systems, they too can become successful investors.

We have house tours where we walk people through a house and explain what we're doing with that particular house, what work is being done, how we raise the money, and why we're doing what we're doing in that home.

We have a cash flow game night where we play the game 'Cash Flow' by Robert Kyisoki. From this game, individuals are able to learn that it doesn't matter what they do for a living or how much money they make, everyone can become financially free by using the strategies taught in the game.

Shannon:

How has your education in real estate changed the way you invest?

Richard:

I used to think the way to make money in real estate was trying to qualify for a bank loan and then fix and flip a house. I didn't realize how many strategies there are to make money in real estate investing.

As I educated myself, I implemented some cool strategies. I've been able to pick up 17 doors that pay me monthly. The best part is I didn't use any of my money or credit to buy those homes.

Shannon:

What is one of the top real estate strategies you have learned?

Richard:

How to raise money. Learning this one strategy has allowed me to do transactions that I wouldn't have been able to do otherwise. This strategy helped me buy more homes without having to go to a bank to get a loan or to qualify for a loan.

Another strategy called "velocity banking" has helped me get out of debt faster. With the doors that I have right now, if I really wanted to expedite it I could have those doors pay themselves off in the next 12 months.

By implementing what I learned from raising money and velocity banking, incredible things have happened for my family. In less than three years I will have gone from 1 door to 17 doors, and they will be paid for free and clear. Those rentals will then pay me the rest of my life!

Shannon:

What is the number one mistake an individual makes when buying their first investment property?

Richard:

Not being educated in real estate investing. There's not a ceiling to how much money you can make, and there's no floor either. Individuals think doing real estate transactions are really easy. You buy it, then turn around and sell it, and you're going to make money. I think too many people over the years miscalculate their numbers. They don't account for varying factors that could take place in a real estate transaction.

Then, unfortunately, the next thing you know they're losing all their money. They've lost their credit. They've lost their home. Now they have a really bad taste in their mouth about real estate investing. One of my mentors told me once, "If you think education is expensive, try ignorance." That's the one thing that stops so many people—their ignorance to the fact that they need to be educated. They need to learn how to go out and successfully close on transactions because, if you successfully close on one transaction, you can successfully close on two, three, and so forth. If they don't know what they're doing, one real estate transaction could put them out of the game for the rest of their life. Applied education is key.

Shannon:

How have mentors in your real estate investing helped you get educated for potential pitfalls?

Richard:

When I'm able to ask my mentors questions, they can walk me through step by step of what I need to do. That's been a huge advantage for me. If I can't call them, or get in contact with them, I could make a very costly mistake. By being able to have those mentors that I can contact, they can walk me through that land mine so I don't make costly mistakes. That, to me, is absolutely priceless. I'm able to learn from their successes. I'm able to learn from their failures. I'd rather learn from their failures than from my failures. That's the big thing with mentors. They're there to mentor us, to assist us, to make sure that we're able to go out and be successful real estate investors.

Shannon:
How does learning multiple investing strategies protect and accelerate investing success?

Richard:
The advantage of being able to have multiple strategies is when I talk to a homeowner I can learn more about their situation and what they need. Instead of being focused only on one strategy, I can now evaluate their current situation and give them multiple ways on how we can best serve them. By giving them multiple options, this allows me to pick up more homes and, in turn, make more money.

Shannon:
What is the best strategy for finding transactions?

Richard:
Honestly, word of mouth. Letting people know you're in business. The biggest mistake that I see people make is they get into real estate but no one knows it. They open the door, but the lights are turned off and no one is talking. People need to know what we do. People need to hear, "Hey, I'm in real estate, if you know anyone that might be selling their home or might be in financial trouble with their home, let me know."

Property management companies, they manage a lot of properties. Their homeowners will come to them and say, "Hey, I want to get rid of this property." Or, "Hey, we've come upon financial troubles and we need to get rid of this property. Do you have any ideas?" We can leverage property management companies. We can go to different networking events and work with different attorneys.

Just get out and talk to people. The more people who know you're in business, the more transactions you're going to pick up.

Shannon:

When you began your real estate investing career, how important was it for you to establish a team to help you be successful?

Richard:

It's very important. The biggest puzzle piece I put in place has been a great real estate attorney, CPA, and a bookkeeper. Too many times people get overwhelmed on just knowing how to set things up and have little idea about how much they do or don't have to pay in quarterly taxes. They think they can run the numbers themselves but that can be very stressful and overwhelming. My team keeps me on track, and I'm not stressing and worrying around tax season! Now I can keep the majority of my income and keep all of my cash flow!

Shannon:

What is cash flow and why is it such an important part of your business?

Richard:

Cash flow is what I take home above and beyond any of the expenses of that rental property. For example, on one of my properties, rent is $1,200 a month, my mortgage is $600, my property management fees, taxes, insurance, and bookkeeping total approximately $300 a month. I have $300 positive cash flow off that property. Once that property is paid off, I'll be cash flowing closer to $900 on that home each month! I really like other people paying off my mortgages and making me wealthier each month.

See, there's a myth that we've been taught since we were kids, where we have to be at least 62 to 65 to retire. The majority of us have been taught that we have to work 40 hours a week for 40 years to then retire on 40 percent of what we have been accustomed to making. I hated that idea! I wanted to be able to retire younger and wealthy. I realized that if I made $10,000 passively a month and my monthly bills were $6,000 and I was 40 years old I was retired, after all of my monthly bills were paid I still had $4,000 left over!

That's what I loved about real estate investing and the strategies Renatus teaches. Get massive income through multiple strategies and then turn that into passive income. When we do this, life becomes a lot easier. We don't have the stress. We're now able to become a better husband, a better father, a better provider, a better wife, a better spouse, a better brother, a better sister. That's what I love about having that cash flow—it's extra money that comes in every single month. When my wife and I got married, we got married to be together, not to be apart all of the time. When we have that cash flow coming in, we're able to experience life on a different level.

That's the big thing for me with real estate investing, and why I love it so much. We have the opportunity. If we go out and we're willing to work and we're willing to put in the time, the effort, and the energy, we can be retired in the next five to seven years if we want. I don't have to wait until I'm a certain age. For me, when it comes to investing that's what I focus on. I wanted to get out of debt! I wanted to be able to have that cash flow coming in as soon as I could so we can travel the world. We can go out and live the life that we want to on our terms, instead of having to live life on the terms our employer or our boss has set up for us.

Shannon:
What type of legacy do you want to leave?

Richard:
There's a couple things. A legacy of hard work and ethics! For my kids, it's important to me that they know no matter how tough things got, Dad never gave up. I want to be able to leave a legacy that if my kids ever were to Google my name, nothing negative ever came up on the internet.

A legacy of giving back. Through one of our community members we are setting up water wells and giving villages electricity! I'm able to make a difference in individuals lives that I will never meet personally.

I want to leave a legacy of knowledge for my kids. If they go out and apply the knowledge that we have, that they can be free the rest of their lives.

I want to be able to put my kids in a position where they know the importance of helping others. The more we've been blessed, the more we need to give back and help others.

When I die, I don't want to have 20 people show up at my funeral. Because of the impact I've been able to have on other people's lives, there are thousands of individuals that I hope show up. When my boys meet them that it's not, "Your dad helped me make so much money." Instead, "Your dad made a difference in my life. Your parents were able to do these things for us." It is that legacy of helping, living way below our means, to be able to help and bless other individuals have a better life so that their legacy, their family tree, can be forever changed. When I had no money, when I had no credit, when I felt like a failure as a husband and father because I couldn't make our monthly payments, I made a choice to go out and do something different.

I decided to stand up and not settle. I wanted to go out and create something through hard work, passion, and devotion. Our children's lives are different because we went out and got to work, and had a passion for being able to help and serve other people to make their lives better.

Joshua White

Joshua White is an accomplished entrepreneur, real estate investor, published author, and motorsport professional. He is CEO and Founder of R3 ENTERPRISES LLC and Projects Motorsport LLC.

Joshua's hobbies include Pro-racing, travel, and creating memories with family. He is the father of a wonderful teenage daughter, Madelynn Grace. Armed with only an Associates of Science degree, Joshua has managed to break through the dogma and fodder of society and become a great success in real estate investing and Pro motorsports, while helping others do the same. Relationships and family are the foundation of Joshua's approach to his life. He is currently on the path to retiring from his business and is creating a long lasting legacy for himself, his friends, and his family.

Contact Info:
Joshwhiterealestate@gmail.com
Owner and CEO of R3 ENTERPRISES LLC

Shannon:
What inspired you to get into real estate?

Josh:
I worked in landscaping and irrigation installing for some pretty wealthy people. I was also a firefighter. A lot of the top brass invest in real estate simply because they know that the retirement they're going to receive is not going to be sufficient for the way they want to live. Also, as I was installing water features in elaborate landscapes, no matter what they did as a profession: doctor, lawyer, super sales person, anything they all had one thing in common. They all invested in real estate. That is what opened my eyes about 10 years ago. I knew that I wanted to be in the real estate world.

Shannon:
When you were in their homes did any of them offer up advice?

Josh:
First, they told me that real estate has been working for thousands of years. Second, they told me if you were to investigate true wealth in this country (not just being rich as rich and wealth are two different things), every single one of them has their hand in real estate.

Shannon:
Did any of them give you specific advice?

Josh:
Rentals. Start getting rentals, start acquiring rentals at least one or two a year.

That is the new retirement. You need to have investments in real estate because real estate is insured and backed by the real estate. I'm not going to talk bad about the stock market but nothing there is insured. It is a great way to make money if you know what you're doing but nothing is insured. It could crash tomorrow and everybody's money is lost. With real estate the worst case scenario is that you own the property.

Shannon:

They make it sound so easy, "Rentals, acquire one or two a year." That sounds super simple, but how do you do that?

Josh:

There's many different strategies you have to be able to execute to actually have a property become a rental. You can buy it at a deep down discount and it can need a lot of work. When you're done with it, you have a choice to sell it or keep it and it would become an asset. You need to know a few different strategies to execute that but it all comes down to knowledge and education.

Shannon:

What is the first piece of advice you would give someone who is just starting off in investing?

Josh:

It would be from a tax and legal point, get yourself structured to do real estate. There's many different entity structures in this country and many different types of entities and protection. You need to understand the business under the business before you even start out in real estate. That is asset protection, the way credit works and the way the tax is structured. You need to get your own tax structure tailored to you and what you're going to do, not what somebody else tells you to do. The best way to do that is have an interview with a CPA or an attorney and figure out what you're going to do with real estate. That is the first advice I'll give you.

Josh:

That's the important part. Doing real estate without any of these structures is like getting in a Ferrari with no motor in it and trying drive 100 mph.

You need to start with the first nut and the first bolt and you need to put those two together, and then you go get the next nut and the next bolt. Or if not, you're going to take off and you're going to fall apart.

Shannon:

Is real estate investing success depended on a strong economy?

Josh:

No. There are different strategies for different times in the market. You can make money in a down-market, you can make money in an up-market, all it takes is knowledge. You need to know the different strategies.

Shannon:

What is a good strategy in a down-market if you want to create massive income?

Josh:

A lot of people in the down-market get overstretched during the time and then it crashes. They get overleveraged on their homes and that's when the foreclosures start. A lot of mortgage companies want you to believe that you can afford the home but you really can't. In a down-market, foreclosures and short sales are the strategy.

The best thing I like about the down-market is you can really, really help people massively and also make massive money. In a foreclosure, you can help them get out of that home or help them save that home. If you help them get out, you can acquire the home. Help them and deal with them to acquire the home, keep a foreclosure off of their life and credit. What you've actually done is help them and you've acquired a home for a deep-discount before the bank even got to look at it.

Shannon:

How do you find those people? Is it easy?

Josh:

Well, you can find a list. It's an NOD list or notice of default. You have to create relationships to get them. Good relationships with real estate agents or real estate brokers are essential.

Another thing in a down-market with a foreclosure is rentals. Since a lot of people are getting foreclosed on they need a place to live. You could help them with their home and if you own a big building, you could say, "Well, I have a place you can go." You're getting the transaction on the home plus you're getting the business for your rental. You're helping them in two different facets.

Shannon:

It sounds to me like, really, taking care of the people is almost just as important as making money in real estate. Is that accurate?

Josh:

It's more important. The money is a receipt. The money, at least in my business, is result of what I do and is secondary. A good investor is a problem solver. Every transaction is a problem where it wouldn't be for sale, so you find the problem in there and you try to solve the problem. That's how you become successful, the money comes. If you do it for money, some things will work out, some things won't. I tried to model myself after helping first and get the compensation later.

Shannon:

What is the difference between wealthy people and rich people?

Josh:

Rich people are usually fast new money, lottery-type people, people that win this, win that. They might find a good product and they'll start a business and sell it and make a lot of money and go out and buy a lot of cars. That's rich people. It's the education that's the difference between rich and wealthy. Wealthy people have knowledge and their education is a journey. For rich people, their education stopped at college or stopped at the knowledge they have before they came up with their product and then it stopped and they're just rich. Wealth is something different. Wealth is people thinking of the back side of life versus the front of your face side. It's a different mindset and it takes a little bit coaching to get that, plus a lot of personal insight and wanting to learn and develop to get that away.

The true wealth in this country didn't happen 10 years ago, it happened 60, 70 years ago. The Rockefellers, the Morgans, and Carnegie. That's when wealth started, true wealth. If you find true wealth, if you date it back and you research, it started a long time ago and it's compounding. One thing that makes it clear to me is we say, "Wealth of knowledge" not "Rich of knowledge."

Shannon:
How important do you think it is to have a mentor in real estate?

Josh:
It's vital. It's a team sport. Real estate and investing, it's all a team sport. To do it alone is downright reckless.

Shannon:
Why?

Josh:
Because it's all about relationships. To do it yourself, you're kind of a loner, a shadow. You can do it but it's the relationships that help you gain the good projects and the good deals.

Shannon:
Do you read books on personal development?

Josh:
I read lots of books.

Shannon:
What is your favorite book that you've listened to this year?

Josh:
The Creature from Jekyll Island.

Jekyll Island is south of the Georgia coast and all the guys that met there, from Charles Schwab, J. P. Morgan, to Carnegie, that's how the Federal Reserve was born. A lot of things were very maddening but a lot of things, through getting frustrated, make sense now. Now, I understand the history of currency. It's crazy when you read that book. Every day of your life, you watch things pass your face that come from that book. It's great knowledge to have, to know the history of money. If you want to be really good in investing in real estate, find the history of money first.

I drive race cars. They say I'm a basket case before I get my car, but when I get my car and go 200 miles an hour and everybody says they feel like I'm asleep because I calm down. I calm down when there's chaos. At 200 miles an hour, cars all around me, that's my happy spot—I wish I could do my classes in the middle of a race.

I have to listen to my team and my spotter on the radio. I have to know what's going on around me and he does that because I can't turn around to watch.

Shannon:
How are race cars similar to real estate?

Josh:
They go hand in hand. Like I said, if you build your Ferrari without a motor, are you going to go very far? You got to build it from the inside. A Ferrari is really ugly if you take the shell off and you can look inside of it—it's like a robot. That's what you have to build before you put your shell on. Then after the shell, you're sexy and you're ready to go.

Shannon:
Are you only doing properties in Utah or investing nationwide?

Josh:
In Washington also. I'm going to get a couple of flips going there, there is a lot of opportunity up there.

Yeah. If you got a roof that has an issue here, you better get it done this week because if you let it go, you just take the value of your house down because it just gets worse and worse. If it gets in the walls, you're really done because then you got black mold.

Black mold is bad for your health. Banks don't like it. It's toxic, it's a biohazard, grows pores in your lungs.

On the extent of it. It also has a lot to do with your contractor. You look to your contractor: is this fixable in our budget? If he says yes, then we go with it.

Shannon:
What is your best strategy for finding fix and flips?

Josh:
Drive for dollars. I like to drive around. I like to find the neighborhoods that I like, and I like to drive around. There are other places that you can search for them; you can go to the city or county building. Again, that's another relationship that we have to create in real estate. There are lots of brokers out there; you need to get in the network, and the relationships are where it starts.

Shannon:
It sounds to me like the brokers and the real estate agents have all of these advantages, why wouldn't you just get your real estate license?

Josh:
Because a real estate license means taxes and legal. If I am going to do a deal, I go get an agent or a broker. The agent's job will be to get all the paperwork done and keep it right concerning taxes and legalities, keep everything legal. Now, if you go and get a real estate license and you're a registered federal real estate agent, there are parts of investing that you cannot do and it limits you.

Shannon:
Do the realtors help you with short sales?

Josh:
Yes.

Shannon:
What is the MLS and why wouldn't you want to buy a house off of something that sounds so official?

Josh:

The MLS is the Multiple Listing Service, it's where homes go to be sold. A lot of times, it's where homes go after everybody looks at them and they're not a deal anymore. They go on the MLS so everybody can see them.

Shannon:

Do most people buy off the MLS or do they know that they should dig?

Josh:

Some people do, some people don't. I know a friend that can find a deal off the MLS in about 15 minutes.

Shannon:

You should have him teach you that.

Josh:

I'm in the process, or I can just employ him to do that—he's one of my friends and business partners. He's good at it so I let him do that. I'm good at other things.

Shannon:

It's interesting you say that. When you're doing a fix and flip, how much of the work do you do yourself?

Josh:

Absolutely zero.

Shannon:

Is that because you don't know how?

Josh:

No, I do know how, but if I was to go and install a window and do it wrong, in order to get that fixed, I have to go talk to myself in the mirror and tell myself to fix it. If I have a professional do it, it's also guaranteed. If I do it, it's not guaranteed, it's not insured. I go and get a license and bonded insured professionals to do the work.

Josh:

You spend more money doing the work yourself because you're spending not only the money but you're spending your time. If I were doing what we're doing, we're using money as the tool and time is the reason. Right?

Shannon:

Yeah. Do you think it's ever beneficial to do the work yourself?

Josh:

There's things you can do, like fixtures. If I have an afternoon, I'll go in and help my contractor. I'm not the boss, the contractor is the boss. I'll go in and do fixtures and do handles. I like to learn how to do that stuff, put up a blind, stuff like that, paint. The stuff that needs tools and the stuff that needs craftsmanship, I let other people do that, and I like to hire them and I like to put food on their table.

Shannon:

Nice. Short sales, are you comfortable talking about short sales?

Josh:

Been involved in a couple. It's not a short sale, it should be called the long purchase, I know that.

Shannon:

Okay. Why? How long will it take? I thought they were supposed to be short.

Josh:

No. The word short is shorting the bank on the price, that's the meaning for short.

You're trying to talk to the bank to come up with a price and it's usually short of the actual price. They're trying to get it off their books. See, banks don't want these homes on their books because they have to pay taxes on them, so they will short sale it to you to get it off their portfolio.

Shannon:

Is there a common percentage or a dollar amount that you should go offer the bank when you are going in to try and get a short sale?

Josh:

It's all situational, location and type of property. Now, short sales are going down as a strategy right now.

Shannon:

Why?

Josh:

Because we're going to try to get the short in the bank but now since, I don't know, 2010, 2011, we have depreciation, correct? The banks can't short them this much now because it's depreciated. Understand?

Shannon:

Do you find the short sales on that MLS list?

Josh:

Yes, you can. I have an agent up here in Seattle that has her own brokerage but she works for the bank so she has this whole file cabinet full of these short sales that aren't even on the MLS. They're in a file cabinet. I call her up and say, "Hey, I need a couple of rehabs to do," she'll go into her file and she'll pull one out.

Shannon:

Well, that should be interesting especially doing it in Seattle. How much time do you think you'll need to spend up there?

Josh:

Well, I have my sister there and she is a brand new real estate investor. She is going to take care of a lot of the marketing up there and find some stuff. I'm just going to be going back and forth from Utah. I'm not doing any rehabs in Utah right now, I'm looking to do them up there because I'm teaching my sister this game.

Shannon:
I love that you just called it a game; why did you refer to it as a game?

Josh:
Because it's fun and you constantly have to practice and you constantly have to perform—you can't get complacent. You can sit on the sidelines or you can jump in, it's a choice.

Shannon:
Love it. Your goal is to always win the game?

Josh:
Well, not always win the game but always play well, how about that?

Shannon:
I like that. That's a concept we're teaching our kids right now. It's not about winning and losing, it's how you play the game.

Shannon:
What type of legacy do you want to leave?

Josh:
I want to leave a legacy of honesty and, first of all, responsibility. I want to be known as a person that practiced responsibility and honesty. I want to leave a legacy to teach young kids how to create wealth and how to not have to depend on church, family, state, government. One of my biggest things is I want to create entrepreneurial schools for children. That's one of the legacies I want to leave—knowledge and education for young children.

Marsha Yearian

Marsha Yearian founded Monte Fe Investments Management & Consulting LLC in 2014 as a real estate investment and asset management firm with a focus on self-storage investing through a subsidiary company, Monte Fe Self Storage Series B LLC. Marsha organizes and manages investor groups that purchase million-dollar self-storage businesses. These businesses are improved and expanded on a three to five-year exit plan. During the ownership period, Marsha is responsible for overseeing the on-site management team and operations of each self-storage business. In addition to self-storage, Marsha is a multi-family investor, note buyer, and organizer of Meetups REI-Just More Zeros and Real Estate Investors of Texas. The meetups attracted individuals wanting to become real estate investors which pivoted Marsha to look for an education solution for these "newbie" investors. Early in 2017, Marsha was introduced to the Renatus Nation by Ryan Dodge. This provided the education solution for new investors and sparked Marsha's interest and understanding of how to invest in residential real estate.

In addition to her real estate asset management business, Marsha owns and operates aNetBIZ, an internet business development company that has been in operation since 2002. Her professional experience includes website development, hosting server tech support, search engine optimization specialist, internet marketing, and social media branding. Marsha's focus on bringing the vision into reality has resulted in creating successful businesses both for her clients and herself.

Prior to 2002, Marsha owned a remodeling company for over 10 years, managing all aspects of the business and sub-contractors including designing and developing construction plans.

Shannon:

It seems like you are already doing some real estate investing, not residential though.

Marsha:

I haven't gone in the direction of residential yet; however, the Renatus education system is quickly changing that. I became involved in real estate investing a little bit differently due to some personal experiences. A number of years ago, when homes were being foreclosed on, I happened to have family members who personally experienced that situation. In fact, one of the family members didn't fall behind on payments at all. The mortgage companies in selling to one mortgage company after another lost track of payments and it was something that even three different lawyers could not get corrected. The mortgage companies had closed or been bought out. Tracking records was impossible. Finally, in frustration, loan modifications were set in place and all monies claimed to be owed were added into the loan. We just gave up the fight. That was my mother's house, so I was the one who was communicating with all entities to correct the issues. This experience developed my interest in real estate investing; however, it made me cautious about the residential market. Instead I researched for statistically proven safer real estate areas.

At that point in time, I was successfully helping clients develop internet businesses. I wasn't looking for a new career. I could work from home, set my own hours, and still enjoy family activities and vacations anytime. Also it was quite a bit of fun to have money deposited into bank accounts overnight from the sale of web services or affiliate marketing.

The mortgage problems taught me the steps that people needed to take in order to save their home from foreclosure and created a strong interest in real estate. I started taking a look at the markets. Then, one thing led to another. I founded a company with two friends; however, after a few months, one of them moved away out of state and the other had a full-time business that she choose to concentrate on. So I ended up with a real estate company thinking I was going to concentrate on helping those caught up in foreclosure.

Before long I began to realize that maybe the foreclosure industry wasn't really where I wanted to go. I have a lot of friends who are successful in residential investing; however, my personal experience of foreclosure made me nervous about this area. I began to look at other forms of real estate investing, like apartments, commercial buildings, retail spaces. Then all of a sudden I had sticker shock; everything I was looking at was a million dollars or more. I was like, "Oh, my! How am I going to do that?" One thing led to another, and I ended up in self-storage acquisitions. When I looked at the stats on self-storage, it did not crash, or it didn't go down like the housing market did. So I had my goal!

The self-storage industry was making progress from 2008 to 2011, it was steadily showing an increase. Careful research and self-storage training at workshops and online convinced me that self-storage investing would become my goal. My next thing was how to fund as I am "unfundable" since I had been paying cash for everything and am debt-free. I realized there were people all over the United States that preferred having someone find properties, take care of due diligence, and put everything together in reports, proforma projections, development plans and then they would become passive investors. Anyway, that's how I started as a real estate investor in 2014.

Shannon:
Must be nice, passive investors.

Marsha:

Yes! Working with passive investors in self-storage acquisitions is nice but still with challenges, as you have to develop private placement offerings and follow SEC guidelines. In June 2017, I bought in with two other investors an apartment building. In July 2017, with another investor group, we bought land to build a multi-purpose development project from the ground up. The first self-storage project was an existing cash flowing business with four acres to expand into. Anyway, I guess you can tell you got me started talking about my passion.

Shannon:

No, that's perfect. You actually answered a ton of questions in that.

Marsha:

Well, whenever I finally decided that I wanted to buy a self-storage facility, I looked at some numbers, and I figured out what size of a facility I would have to buy in order to make good profit plus it was not my goal to end managing one daily. Operating and managing remotely was the target. That put me into needing to buy facilities in the million-dollar range. So now without having a million dollars and being "unfundable" credit wise I had to find the money people.

I discovered a gentleman by the name of Scott Meyers. I had checked him out in the internet world. Being in the internet world I see a lot of guru training, and I didn't really want to go that route. I wanted to make sure that I went with someone who had their feet on the ground and was truly working what they were teaching, not just making a lot of money teaching people how. Scott fit that criteria.

I went to his private money summit with one of my first partners and met a lot of people and that's when I came to the realization that there were people in that room that could help with buying facilities.

Again I am someone who has always paid cash for everything. I don't have a real high credit score as a result. You know it's a two-edged sword if you don't buy things on credit and keep a lot of credit accounts open that you're paying on every month. Your credit rating's is not that great. I literally did not have any credit or any money to buy a facility nor did I have the self-storage management background that investors would be prefer to see. Definitely was not of interest to any bank. Someone once told me that banks are great when you do not need them. What I had was a dream, prayer, and determination to overcome.

Before going to the summit, I visited the Texas Self Storage Association. On the website was a forum where I discovered a 'for sale by owner' who lived out of state. In the process of talking with them, I actually got it under contract so when I went to the private money summit, I had the facility under contract with a closing a couple of months from that time. Just knew my problems were solved! I was going to a private money summit to meet people who would fund my dream. LOL!

In the crowd there were quite a few highly experienced investors that more or less told me that they thought that us two ladies were a little bit crazy thinking we could buy the facility using other people's money. We were told that our best course of action would be to get financing from a bank. As much as possible I wanted to buy facilities using other people's money. Not because I needed their money but because of the things that I saw with what happened with the mortgage industry. I just think it's time that average people have a chance to make a lot of money instead of always going to the banks. A little bit of a renegade there and I don't know that you want to print that.

Shannon:
Of course we do. We want to put out everything about you, so go ahead.

Marsha:
Okay. I really wanted to do something that would allow people to make money and so when these experienced investors in that crowd told us what the smartest thing we could do was, well, I'm single. My friend was not. She's married. They pretty much said, "You two ladies need to go back to Texas and you need to get your husbands to go sign a loan so you can buy your facility and then once you buy it, then you can find people with money." I've been a single mom, and I've raised seven children without child support. I've gone against the odds many, many times. Whenever this gentleman said that, I didn't realize it, but well the people in the audience said, I kind of

clenched my fists and I stepped forward and said, "Sir, you don't know the women from Texas."

I left there determined to prove him wrong and without any investors. We did not ask my friend's husband to go sign. Although he did offer and he did go down and talk to the bank but we just wanted to do it our way, which was a good thing because it was shortly after that my friend said her business was taking so much of her time, so she had to make a choice. She didn't feel like she could do justice to both. I'm very thankful that we didn't take the easy road because she did have to go on and do her own thing and I certainly wouldn't have wanted to be tied up or have them tied up in something that was more my dream.

I came home a bit disappointed because I had this contract and I really thought it was the right thing. We actually never did buy that facility, although we had it under contract three different times. It just turned out not to be the right one.

Somewhere through all of this I came to the realization that investors in my area were not involved much in self-storage investing because they just had not given it much thought. It is not a "sexy" form of investing. At parties, you get more attention if you are an apartment investor. There weren't people talking about self-storage investing when I went to local investor meetings. So I started an investor meetup with a focus on self-storage investing, called REI Just More Zeros (sticker shock experience).

We began meeting every Wednesday at noon. The meetup was for educational purposes only. Getting to know people through the meetup who had family and friends looking for investments led to bringing a couple of people onto my team so that there were five of us putting the first deal together. That gave us a lot of credibility. We raised enough money and bought our first income producing self-storage facility with room for expansion. The dream materialized without using credit and bank financing.

Shannon:
That's awesome.

Marsha:

Yeah. It's been a really great experience with a learning curve but isn't everything? A lot of challenges, trials and some failure but correcting the course as we traveled.

Shannon:

Success is you learn from your failures so that's I think very common. How important do you feel that it is to establish a good team? You talked about how you went through several different "partners." They didn't end up being partners, but it sounds like then you established a team. How important do you feel now. if you were starting over, is it to have a good team and why?

Marsha:

From the investor standpoint, it was for credibility and to make sure that the investor's reliance was not just on one person handling their money. It was to give them confidence. For me, it was important to have a team with skills, background, and experience different from mine. If you are going to use other people's money, you want to be sure about your plans and projections. It takes many eyes to see all aspects of a project. Others may not be so in love with the "dream" that they cannot see the warts.

I thoroughly enjoy doing web development, and I don't necessarily want to give that up. I'm continuing to do that as well. I have a doctor who wrote a book. I've been helping her for about three and a half, maybe four years now with getting her book out there into the marketplace. I like creating businesses I guess you could say. I don't want to give that up. That means having a team because otherwise you're going to have to be the one there every single day onsite making sure things happen right or managing the property.

Shannon:

Which is not something you want to do because you want your income to be passive, correct?

Marsha:

Right, right. Passive income building real estate equity and increasing a cash flowing business for resale is the exit strategy. We found a gentleman who manages that property for us and he does a super, super, super good job. A lot of times there's people right in the neighborhood that just need a part time job or a few hours that will come and work at your facility. It works out real well. That's what I'd hoped to achieve. It is something that has a place for anyone that becomes connected with it to be blessed by it, I guess you could say.

Shannon:

Perfect.

Marsha:

The investors, I want them to make money. I want to be able to give people in the local area jobs so that they can earn that extra money they might need or maybe they don't want to drive too far, they want to be able to work close to home. The self-storage industry is an industry where controlling your bottom line from year to year is easy. Your expenses don't change that much, so it's much easier to judge what your profit is going to be. Every month there's money left at the end of the month above your expenses. That money goes to our investors until they reach a certain level and then to us as developers.

Anyway, we're building equity in real estate. We're also taking a business that maybe wasn't performing at its full potential, building it up and then we can turn around and sell it in a few years.

Shannon:

Perfect. How has your education in real estate changed the way that you're investing?

Marsha:

My education in real estate, how did it change it? Well, I guess because I didn't jump off into the guru training that I saw in the internet world. When I first thought about going into the foreclosure market, there was a lot of gurus out there that had training programs that were going to teach me how to make millions overnight. I just wasn't comfortable with that, being in the internet world like I am. Finding Scott helped me to become focused on self-storage so that changed my direction in the real estate investing world to begin with; however, I am becoming diversified.

Finding Renatus, though, has restored my hope for getting into the residential market. More importantly, the Renatus program provides a way for beginning investors to earn money as they learn. I like that! Many that come to my meetup are not ready for the long-term investing that self-storage is. They need money NOW! That is how Renatus helps meet that need. I am an entrepreneur! For dreams to come true, lifestyles to be lived by choice, I believe everyone needs to be one.

Shannon:
Perfect. Let's touch on that a little bit. What is your favorite strategies or the best strategies that you have learned about residential real estate investing that you want to use?

Marsha:
Mortgage Acceleration and the tax/business entities strategies. I also want to start buying raw land.

Shannon:
Okay.

Marsha:
I'm looking at raw land because there's a lot of people who don't have strong enough credit to build a house or to buy a house. If I buy the land, I can turn around and finance the land for them. This may allow them a "hand up" in reaching the goal of owning their home. Paying for land can be more affordable within their budget. At least they could have something visual that provides stronger belief in reaching their goal.

Shannon:
So you'd find the land?

Marsha:

Yes. I've started looking for raw land. What I will do is owner finance the land.

Shannon:

Oh, perfect. Okay.

Marsha:

It's raw land maybe through tax sales.

Shannon:

Let's continue on this. You said that you find the raw land. Most of them are tax liens.

Marsha:

Right.

Shannon:

You make it sound really easy. In laymen's terms, or in more complex terms, whichever ones you want, what is a tax lien and how can you own the land and then seller finance it if you just have a tax lien?

Marsha:

If there's tax liens on the property and it's going to auction you can track down the owner of the land and you can offer to buy it by cleaning up liens and maybe giving them more if it is worth it.

You track down the owners through the internet. A lot of times it's land that maybe somebody has inherited so they let it get behind for whatever reason. You come in and save their credit by offering to catch the tax lien up but, of course, they're selling the land to you first. In other words they're turning it. I do work with attorneys as part of my team as well. You find the property, find the seller, make arrangements, make an agreement to where you're catching up the taxes but at the same time they are selling that land to you. Prior to closing make sure there are not any liens on the land or allow for them being settled at closing. Then once you own the land, owner finance it to someone else.

Shannon:

So do you drive around the city and look for empty pieces of property?

Marsha:

No, not necessarily. I do a lot of that through the internet. I contact county offices and get their tax rolls. Again, anything I can do from my home office online, that's what I'm going to do. I contact county offices. But my eyes are always open when driving for possibilities. Love the iPhone for making pics of 'for sale fast and easy.'

Shannon:

That's what I want you to elaborate on. You just get on the internet. You contact the county office and they say, "Oh, here's a whole bunch of properties that have tax liens on them." Is that accurate?

Marsha:

I ask them for a list. Some of them will want to charge me for the list and some of them will send me the list for free or maybe a very nominal fee. As long as the list is not more than $25, maybe $50 if I think it's a really good area, then I will buy it. Then it's a matter of mailing. Here's something interesting to me, I can do mail outs to self-storage owners and I get great results and I can do mail outs to people that are in trouble with taxes or have some kind of liens on their property and I get good results for that. They're seeing me as somebody that is going to solve a problem. Self-storage owners, maybe they're tired. Maybe they've been running that business themselves and been physically there whatever hours they're open for the public and they're just ready to retire. Those two forms of marketing to these types of lists work. Then I just respond to the ones that send back replies.

I've had a situation with a family member where we had a difficult time financially and not necessarily my family member's fault. It was just something that happened and I learned a lot. Now I'm still working with people. Even a tax lien in a way, that it is a foreclosure. I'm still working with people in that area to help as many people as I can. If they're interested in maybe selling the property, we'd be glad to settle the lien and take it off their hands and they'll be done with it. Save their credit. Sometimes they're embarrassed, feeling like they did something wrong but they really didn't. The circumstance may be beyond their control. Or maybe they made a mistake and they know it! They just need a way out that is not embarrassing.

Shannon:
That works for you? That seems to work well?

Marsha:
Yes. Now, as far as the apartment building, it was with the gentleman who brought me into Renatus and he found it on Craig's List. I knew people that were looking for apartments to buy and so we put it together.

Shannon:
Nice. When you're looking for multifamily dwellings, what's one of the first things that you look out for?

Marsha:
Well, I actually don't look for multifamily. I look for self-storage. This just happened to be a deal. Because, again, I have this meet up, a lot of people know me. People bring deals to me now. If I can make the connection, I make the connection. Multi-family, that's not a good area for me to talk about because I'm more in favor of self-storage but a deal's a deal. When you find something you can get into with very little money down and that's going to be owner financed, I'm all for that. As long as I can see that there's going to be cash left over at the end of the month. Whenever I can see that, then I'll buy an apartment building.

Shannon:
All right. You had this deal brought to you and I know it's not your niche.

Marsha:
Yes, that's right.

Shannon:
You would not have looked into it and you would not have invested in it if there weren't certain criteria that were met.

Marsha:
Right.

Shannon:
What are some of the other things that you're going to look at other than money being left over at the end of the month? That's not necessarily the only thing, correct?

Marsha:
That's correct. The market area. The market area is extremely important. Is this in an area that real estate is appreciating and how easy will it be to find tenants? Why is the seller selling this apartment building? What is the reason for selling? Is it that the seller's just tired and wants out or is there something going on in the market area? Are there businesses that are closing down or people moving out? Is the neighborhood changing? In this particular case, this apartment building is located in an army town. It's one bedroom apartments so it's something constantly be in demand because of affordability. They might only need it for a year. It was the market area more than anything else in this particular purchase. The fact that it was also owner financed was also an attraction. We didn't not have to go to a bank and we could close quickly. It was easy to buy it with good net operating income (NOI).

The other thing is the state of the building, the repair. In other words you have to be able to see that even if worst came to worst and you had to repair, completely renovate an apartment every month because somebody moved out, knocked a whole in the wall, if those repair bills are still going to allow for profit. Also, are you buying the real estate property below market because you can't afford to buy it at market, not in the apartment industry anyway, because the difference between self-storage and apartments is you cannot as easily control your expenses. You very rarely have tenants that move out and destroy your walls or take all the appliances with them. That doesn't happen in the self-storage industry. It can happen in the apartment.

It's a more high risk situation because you can't control your expenses. If you can add up the income and you can see that over a period of time you're still going to have a cash on cash return, but more importantly if you're buying the real estate below market, you've got an appreciating value to that real estate. In the case of this apartment building, we're going to clean it up a little bit so it's going to be worth more when we sell it.

When you can improve the apartment building, hold onto it for three, four years and you'll find another person who wants it. They like it because now you've improved the building. You've also improved the quality of the tenants. You have a system or a method of how you're doing business and all they have to do is pick it up. It's like a blueprint. All they have to do is step in and continue to follow your blueprint and they can make money. Maybe it's somebody who wants to live in one of the apartments themselves and own the building and have other people paying for it. There's just so many possibilities.

Shannon:
Great. Thank you. What type of legacy do you want to leave?

Marsha:
This might sound a little gruesome but say it's the end of my life and there's a memorial for me and I would like for people to come up and say, "You're mom helped me do this" or "You're mom helped me do that." I would like to know that I was able to help somebody do something that was beyond what they thought they had the ability to do. Buying a million-dollar property when you don't have the credit or the money to do it is beyond what most people think they can do; but it can be done. Through prayer and faith I do it; so they can too.

My Motto: Dream, Believe, Achieve!

Munira Zahabi

Munira Zahabi is the founder and CEO of Kismet Ventures, Inc. She earned her Master's degree in HealthCare Management from California State University in 2007. Munira is an entrepreneur, real estate investor, and internationally John C. Maxwell certified, coach trainer, and speaker. She believes in adding value to people.

She enjoys international travel; she speaks seven languages fluently and is working on Spanish to add to her linguistic skills. Munira enjoys various cultures and building new relationships while cementing the old ones as she ventures out to help people gain a better understanding of the opportunities available by making small changes to their mindsets and habits.

She believes that her work in the healthcare sector has prepared her for empowering people to overcome reservations, and she approaches every facet of her life with enthusiasm and creativity.

Her mission is to encourage people to "Venture Out" and step out of their comfort zone. She believes that the changing business world offers many opportunities for dynamic growth and is looking to inspire & motivate individuals to the next level of prosperity.

Based in Chicago, Illinois, Munira partners with her husband, Mansoor, to build a life that creates positive financial opportunities while allowing time to relax, have fun, and enjoy the grandchildren.

Contact Info:
zahabim@gmail.com
http://www.johncmaxwellgroup.com/munirazahabi/

Shannon:

What inspired you to get into real estate?

Munira:

My father and my grandfather owned real estate in East Africa where I'm from. They owned land and buildings. I was not privy to how they acquired them. They always had issues with tenants, and it seemed a headache because the tenants always seemed to find him at the wrong time. My father advised me that investing in property is valuable, and most of the time the value of the property appreciates. Stuff (to him that meant unnecessary items) doesn't have value and always depreciates. His advice stayed with me.

Shannon:

Does he still own property and real estate in Africa?

Munira:

No, they passed. My grandfather lost his land during the 1964 Zanzibar Revolution, and they had to move to Mombasa, Kenya. They started again and had a few rental properties. My grandfather passed in 1984, and my dad in 1994. We had to liquidate all the assets because my brothers live in the UK, and the USA is my home. So, we left Kenya and decided to leave the ancestral legacy there but start our own across the pond.

Shannon:

When you first came to the United States how did you get started?

Munira:

We lived in someone's home for a month before we got an apartment. By the time the school year ended, we realized we needed a junior high for our oldest child. The rules of the school and bus service were confusing so the hunt for the first home with a good school and pricing requirements began. This resulted in the first move. We moved four times in three years because with four children a good school district was important. Rental properties, we found, were either not the right price, or did not have the schools we wanted in the neighborhood, or both. Our realtor suggested looking at the option of purchasing instead of rental. He showed us the comps and the rent prices and after crunching numbers we came to the conclusion that purchasing a home could be a better option.

And the search for the home began and we found one that everyone liked, there was the question of getting credit. Obtaining credit and building credit was a new concept. In Africa, everything is cash-based. Pay cash and get goods/property. The house we liked was $127K, and the bank approved us for $27,000 mortgage loan. The home we liked was a model home. In the course of finding solutions, I called the builder and asked to speak to him. I left him countless messages and after four months of the same dialog with his staff, he finally agreed to see me. He granted me audience, that one afternoon, after I was on hold on the telephone for over two hours. I met him in his office and explained my situation to him. It took a lot of convincing, and he conceded to hold the note for five years. Little did I know that I was negotiating an "owner financing" strategy.

Shannon:

Well that's amazing. That certainly makes it easier when you come about it naturally.

Munira:

Yes it did come naturally, and we did implement the strategy, but only when I began educating myself did I realize that this was a real estate concept.

Shannon:

So, if someone that you know was going to start in real estate and wanted to get started in real estate, and let's say that maybe they came from

Kenya or maybe they didn't, maybe they just came from Ohio, but they had nothing to get started. What would you recommend that they do first?

Munira:

I would ask them to understand the concepts. This is the foundation. Everybody thinks real estate is easy. I asked acquaintances for advice, and all they said was, "Go buy a house and get a tenant." But it's not easy as it sounds.

The location of the property, all the pertinent information, understanding how to acquire the property, what the deal entails, and how to structure the deal are all important concepts that will give you the upper hand. Without knowledge, a good deal can go bad. So if anybody wants to start, start at the first step. You go to Kindergarten and learn the ABCs, and most importantly the basic concept to build a solid foundation then go from there.

Shannon:

Perfect, so tell me some of the things that you've learned as creative ways to acquire property.

Munira:

I learnt that the 'subject to' means buying a home subject to the existing mortgage.

It means the seller is not paying off the existing mortgage and the buyer is taking over the payments. The unpaid balance of the existing mortgage is then calculated as part of the buyer's purchase price. The buyer now owns and controls the home. The main thing is to make the payments or lose the home to foreclosure.

Shannon:

Have you had a specific example where you've had a mentor help you with a deal that just wasn't for you?

Munira:

I remember when I was trying to invest some money with my bank; they had me fill out an Investor Profile-Risk Assessment questionnaire that helped them understand how much risk I was willing to take with my money.

Mentors are like that. They guide and advise you, and they challenge you to reach your potential. I'm blessed to be part of a local real estate investment community, and I am around a lot of mentors. They do deals every day. They are like the bull dogs and can smell the deals from afar. They gauge you and figure out what your knowledge and comfort level is, and they challenge how much you know. I have not been privileged to have my own deal, but I get to be a part of a group where I am able to listen to a mentor who challenges his students all the time. There are scenarios as well as real deals the students bring in. We slice and dice the deal and come to understand if initial strategy of the deal was the right one or would using another strategy be more effective.

Shannon:
Would you say that you could learn everything from a book from the local library?

Munira:
Libraries are a wealth of information. There's a whole section of real estate books. Some books have a wealth of information and are classics. But one has to be creative to utilize the knowledge from the old books to use it today. Most concepts do not change, but the ingenuity does. Books are outdated, and libraries don't update their books often. Rules change all the time. Real estate, marketing strategies change, funding strategies change, and the real estate rules and regulations change often as the market changes. One has to keep up. There is a lot of material out there; I'm not saying that it should be discounted. But being around the right people, and listening to people who are in the business and doing the business, does make a difference.

Shannon:
That is very true. Sometimes you do, and sometimes you don't.

Munira:
So true. Sometimes you do, and sometimes you don't.

Shannon:

So why do you think people succeed at real estate?

Munira:

People succeed because 1) they have the knowledge and 2) they have a plan with milestones/goal outlined. Studies reveal that those who write down their goals have a much better chance of reaching them than those who don't. What is the amount of money you need to make from real estate investing each month? How many properties do you want to buy? Be specific in what you want to do through real estate. Each goal should be measurable and have a date on it as well. For instance, your goal could be written: "To purchase one investment property in Chicago, Illinois, within the next 90 days."

Shannon:

Okay.

Munira:

You need to have a goal and figure out what you need. First, figure out what kind of properties you're interested in—what's your investment ID? Are you going to fix and hold or fix and flip? How much money you need, how many properties will be enough for you to put you in a good spot. Because you have to look out for yourself first. Set SMART goals—which stand for Specific, Measureable, Attainable, Relevant, and Time-Based. These goals mean you can clarify your ideas, focus your efforts, use your time and resources productively, and increase your chances of achieving what you want in life.

Secondly, understand the market and know the area, because knowing the area will give you the edge. Thirdly, then have an exit plan, because an exit plan will help you either get out of the deal or figure out how to not continue with the deal.

Shannon:

Okay.

Munira:

And fourth, have a great team, because if you have a great team of contractors, people who are on your side—everybody—has a stake in your property. If they have an interest in the property, then it works very well, and it's going to be a profitable. But if somebody does something wrong, then you're going to be upside down and in a lot of trouble.

Finally, periodically go back and look at your plan and see if you need to change or re-adjust your plan, or if you're on target because that's what you have to keep looking for, if you can measure your progress and how you can tweak your plan if you have to.

Shannon:
So would you say being flexible is a key to being successful in real estate?

Munira:
Yes, sometimes it is.

Shannon:
Okay. When do you think that would be successful, and when do you think being flexible might not be?

Munira:
If you find a property, and you go in there thinking, "Oh I'm just going to fix it then flip it," and then as you work on the property you realize this is a good property, that you could put a family in there and make a little bit of passive income on it. Rigid decision making can be brittle in this business. Understanding all strategies are a plus. No deal is just like the previous one. Real estate investing takes time, flexibility, and ambition to make it work well.

Shannon:
So what do you look for when you are looking for a fix and flip?

Munira:
I haven't done one, so I don't think I'm qualified to answer that question.

Shannon:

That's okay; when you do start doing them, what strategies do you think you'll use for finding them?

Munira:

Whatever your investor ID is, you have to partner up with a great agent who will act fast for you and find you deals if you are unable to yourself. Researching prices in the market and rental rates is the key to any deal. Fixing and flipping is a lot more complicated than it appears on TV. There are lots of rules, regulations, and roadblocks that will hinder your ability to make money in this business. To be successful, you must know the rules, this includes buying rules, selling rules, lending rules, construction/permit rules, etc. But most of all I would like to be under an expert's wing. Someone who is a seasoned at doing these deals. Learning from them is like doing a practical within a class in college.

Shannon:

Right.

Munira:

If my investor mentor is successful at completing these deals, then I would rather learn from the best.

Shannon:

Okay. You touched a little bit on passive income. Can you tell me different ways that real estate allows you to earn both passive and massive income?

Munira:

Well massive income will come after you generate a lot of passive income.

Shannon:

Okay.

Munira:

I do not know about massive, but passive income is surely a welcome strategy. You are not dependent on the bi-weekly paycheck and not on your employers' schedule or stuck in traffic. Investing in assets that will generate the income streams, put in the hard work upfront, and reap the benefits as passive income.

Shannon:

Right. Do you have a 1 year, 3 year, and 5 year goal for passive income? For fix and flip or for buying whole properties?

Munira:

Well I haven't planned that far ahead. But I am working on the education, and I plan to learn as I go. My husband and I want to have one rental property by the end of the year.

Shannon:

That's okay, I'm a firm believer in short-term goals.

Munira:

Cool.

Shannon:

Would you like to touch on short sales?

Munira:

My experience with short sales was excruciating. I purchased my condo in Bakersfield, California, in 2005 and was upside down in just two years. I tried loan modification negotiation with the banks, but they would not budge. The loan was sold to three different banks as I tried the short sale proceedings with each bank through a different third party. I was very happy to let the property foreclose after I started the process for the tenth time. Short sales require patience and are arduous. If one is willing to put in the work and have the patience, it would be an ideal investor ID.

Shannon:

Have you read the Forbes article about real estate investing and one of the top three ways people become wealthy?

Munira:

Yes, I read it. The article talks about which Americans rank the richest and which industry they built their wealth in. Real estate is the top third industry.

Shannon:

So as a real estate expert, why do you think that's one of the top three ways that people become wealthy?

Munira:

Because, everybody needs a house.

Shannon:

True.

Munira:

So, there's a saying in my language "Roti, Kapda, aur Makaan." You can wear old clothes and eat left-overs, but you always need a roof over your head.

Shannon:

That is true.

Munira:

It seems that the housing market is booming. This is not happening just in the USA but globally as well: India, Turkey, the Middle East, Africa, and even Australia. Local governments everywhere are eager to improve their communities to attract and retain residents and businesses while maximizing limited resources available for infra-structure needs.

Shannon:

So do you feel like real estate investing success is dependent on a strong economy?

Munira:

Well, yes and no; as an entrepreneurial investor, who wants to become an investor, I don't want the prices of homes to go up. If the economy is weak, the properties are cheaper, which then I can flip or hold and make into a passive income. Nowadays, if you listen to the news, every time they talk about finance it's always about the housing market and how well the market is doing and by what percentage. They won't talk about your 401K. They talk about DOW Index and about the housing market. Finance reports on the radio reported the housing market was up by 5 percent and the Chicago market was up by 7 percent, and the real estate market is doing very well. So that's like a strong economy, but now the banks are careful lending money for mortgages because of the 2008 crash.

Shannon:

That's interesting that you bring up 2008 because here we are looking at all these people who didn't qualify, so now it's much, much harder to get a home loan. So do you know of any creative ways that people can get into a home? Or that you could purchase a home if you were unable to get a home loan?

Munira:

Well I am sure there are other ways; however, one of the strategies I would use is to replicate what the builder did for me. The owner financing strategy! He helped me in my time of need, and I would like to do the same for someone else. It's a win-win situation for both parties.

Shannon:

Great. You mentioned a little bit ago about how they are still building everywhere. We're in America, you're in Chicago, you were in Bakersfield. You talked knowing the market, being from Kenya, and I know that you are now a citizen here, but would you ever do international investing or is that just too many laws, too many loopholes, too many problems?

Munira:

If you have money that's sitting in the bank, invest. It would be a great way to diversify your portfolio and purchase a property, for example in Kenya, and rent it out. Buying real estate in a country other than the one you reside in is a perfect way to truly spread your wealth to ensure you have a real safety net.

However, it may feel like a lot of work if you are doing it alone. You have to have strategies in place and, more importantly, a good team in Kenya to work for you and with you. One thing to keep in mind is to ensure everyone in your team has a stake in it. And remember and follow the 3Ps—Policies, procedures, and protocols of the government.

Shannon:

Oh that's such good advice. Let's go back to just here and local investing. What is cash flow? And why is it so important? Why should it be such an important focus of your business?

Munira:

The short answer is cash flow is the amount of money coming in to a business and the amount of money going out. Think of it as a water tank: water comes in at the top and drains out the bottom. So to keep your tank nice and full, you want more coming in than going out.

Cash is also important because it later becomes payment for things that make your business run: expenses like raw materials, employees, rent, and other operating expenses. Positive cash flow means your business is running smoothly.

Shannon:

Perfect. So, most millionaires and billionaires have investments in both residential and commercial real estate. Why do you think that is?

Munira:

I believe the millionaires may have started out with residential real estate. Then as they learnt the ropes and got more passive income, they dove into commercial.

Residential real estate has relatively low start-up costs. And flipping a property to make the profit is an attractive option, if one does not want to hassle with finding the tenants. The con to real-estate investing is experiencing property management responsibilities, tenants, and other costs if you don't allow the property management company to handle it.

Most commercial properties have an annual return off the purchase price between 6 percent and 12 percent, depending on the area, compared to single family homes which range from 1 percent to 4 percent. The other factor is commercial properties do not bother you once the deal closes. Small business owners generally take pride in their businesses and want to protect their livelihood and maintain and improve the quality of the property and, ultimately, the value of their investment. Residential properties are easier and do not require the larger time commitment, bigger investment, and greater risks of commercial.

To get to the real answer of your question, real estate investing is an investment portfolio and the millionaires invest in both because it adds diversity to the portfolio and spreads out the amount of risk. This strategy could be beneficial during the market fluctuations.

Shannon:
Why is there more risk in commercial real estate?

Munira:
There is risk in the real estate itself. Lack of knowledge can be a risk. Not knowing what to expect can result in unexpected surprises. However, with commercial real estate property management is not easy, there is a chance that a professional property manager will be needed to find the tenants, take care of the legalities, agreements, leases, and daily operations.

Maintaining and upkeep of the property is another factor that adds risk. Commercial real estate requires capital and is capital is tied up. Businesses suffer when there is an economic downturn, and lastly, commercial real estate properties have more visitors. People can get hurt or can damage the property. Vehicular accidents can hit people or damage property and vandalism are big risks.

Shannon:

Perfect. Okay, I wanted to know a little bit more about you. We've gone through most of the official questions, so if you can share, you said you and your brother both left Kenya. He went to the UK, you came to the US. Was there a reason that you chose the US and he chose the UK? Or did they choose you?

Munira:

I was born and raised in Nairobi, Kenya. I moved to Dar-es-Salaam, Tanzania, after my marriage to join my husband. In 1993, I saw the annual ad in the local newspaper announcing the DV-1 visa program and its criteria for application. I followed suit and applied and eight months later received the initial paperwork that stated that I had won the first phase of the lottery.

Shannon:

In Tanzania?

Munira:

Yes. The program allows immigrants from a lot of countries to apply for a visa to the USA. My older brother went to the United Kingdom because he was born days before Kenya got its independence. So at the time of his birth he was a British protected person. Kenya was a British colony before independence. My brother grew up as a Kenyan but was refused a passport, so he left to explore the Queen's country and has been there since.

Shannon:

Nice. So now, do you get to go visit him often?

Munira:

I visited my brothers in early May of this year.

Shannon:

Okay, what does he think of you investing in real estate?

Munira:

I talked to him after he joined the community, and he did not understand what I was doing. We talk real estate and tax strategies that are applicable in USA. He is fascinated with the wealth of knowledge I am gaining.

Shannon:

He sounds smart.

Munira:

Both my brothers are smart and savvy.

Shannon:

Okay. So then, you touched at the beginning about your father and your grandfather and how you left that legacy behind. What kind of legacy do you want to build here, and what do you want to leave behind?

Munira:

Life is a journey. Everyone is going somewhere and our paths cross. Along the way one may find people who will surpass them, some you will leave behind, some will help you along the way for a while. Whatever your path, you may find an angelic personality that will take a chance on you. My path has been difficult, and I have struggled to get to this point. Very few people extended a hand to assist without expecting anything.

I have not reached my destination yet, however, one thing I figured out is there is abundance and plenty to go around. If I give whole-heartedly, it will come back to me. I want people along my path to remember me not because I wanted something from them, but because they understand that I genuinely wanted to assist them along their path. My legacy I want to leave behind is "Every life that I have touched... "

Woody Woodward

Woody Woodward dropped out of high school at age 16, was a millionaire by 26 and flat broke by age 27. After clawing his way out of financial ruin he built four different multi-million dollar companies before he turned 40. Through overcoming this adversity Mr. Woodward has become a best-selling author of fifteen books about turning tragedy into triumph. Having interviewed over 2,500 people around the world for his research, he is the pioneer and founder of *Your Emotional Fingerprint*™. Understanding this cutting edge human technology allows one to strip back the layers of excuses and build a proper foundation for mass achievement in one's personal life, relationships and career. Emotional Fingerprint was chosen as one of the leading techniques to be presented to the United Nations to assist them in reaching their millennial goals.

His latest project is inspiring entrepreneurs with M.O.N.E.Y. Matrix™ daily videos that help them reach their goals, make more money and find fulfillment in their careers. He has shared his cutting edge techniques on ABC, CBS, NBC, FOX and Forbes.

Contact Info:
www.GetMoneyMatrix.com
www.MeetWoody.com

Shannon:

According to Forbes Magazine, real estate is one of the top three ways that people become wealthy. As a real estate expert, why do you feel that this is the case?

Woody:

Real estate is the only investment I know of where you have a tangible, physical product that, even if the market goes down, you can still use. Yes, you can say stocks are tangible, but in reality they're not. Yes, you can lease them out, you can do calls and you can do puts on them, but with real estate, even if the market crashes, you can physically rent that property. You get a tax write-off if you are renting the property; so to me, real estate has always been, looking back in history, one of the top ways to generate revenue.

Shannon:

Do you have an opinion on whether commercial real estate or residential real estate is a better investment?

Woody:

I have friends who do both. I personally have always done residential. As for my friends who do commercial real estate it adds a zero to their net worth. If you're going to make a hundred thousand dollars on flipping a residential property, you'll make about a million flipping a commercial property; so it's the same game, just bigger numbers. If you have the resources to do it, most billionaires do it in commercial property, not residential. A lot of millionaires do residential property.

Shannon:

How hard is it to get started in residential real estate if you don't have a lot of money?

Woody:

That's the great thing about residential versus commercial; it doesn't take hardly anything with residential. Nowadays, you can still put down 3 percent or 5 percent on a home to buy it and then flip it, or to let it appreciate and sell it in the future and make additional revenue by leasing it, or there are a lot of different techniques where you can do owner financing. Owner financing is when the seller can't sell a home, maybe it's a bad market, and they're willing to carry that note for you; so in essence, the seller becomes the bank and you're buying it directly from the seller. You then still have all the legal rights to that property, so you can rent it out, you can fix it up, you can sell it; you can do whatever you want, as long as the seller's paid in full when you sell that home.

Shannon:
When the seller's paid in full, how does that benefit them if they're the bank? How do they buy another house?

Woody:
There is only one of two reasons why a seller will finance, in my experience. First is that they have enough income on their own, but they're happy just to sell it because they want to get a higher interest rate. Right now, if you put your money in the bank, you're going to get maybe 1 or 1.5 percent. If they carry the note on that home for you, they can charge you 5, 7, even 10 percent, so they're making more money on their own money, so they become a bank.

The other reason is that sometimes in a bad market they just can't sell a home. Let's say they owe $200,000 on a home and the home's only worth $175,000, so they physically can't sell it unless they come up with the $25,000 difference; so they'll carry their loan for you, and then as the market changes and goes back up and the home's worth $250,000, you can then sell it and keep that extra $50,000 since you bought it for $200,000. Then they are happy because now they get their $200,000 out that they already owe their bank, and it becomes a little win-win.

Shannon:
When you're actually looking for homes in a down market situation where people are upside down in their homes, do you look at the location? Do you look at the future projections for businesses, neighborhoods, etc.?

Woody:

Absolutely. The number one thing that you hear people always talk about with real estate, the number one technique, is location, location, location. I've had friends who have literally bought corner lots and then they heard that Walmart was coming across the street. This happened to a friend of mind in California who bought the lot for $150,000 and had the owner carry the note. Six months later Walmart announced that they were building across the street. His lot went from $150,000 to $500,000 literally overnight. He would be able to sell that and take that money. Now he can play in the commercial business on a little bit larger level.

Most investor works the same way. You make a little bit, you turn that money over. It's really called compounding interest where you take your principle and your interest and then you roll it over again into the next property. There's also a great tax benefit to that as well. You don't have to pay tax on that money as long as you're rolling it over in to a property of equal or higher value.

Shannon:

What do you think is the number one mistake that an individual makes when buying their first investment property?

Woody:

The number one reason why people make mistakes on their first investment property is they don't have a mentor. They don't have someone to follow. They don't have someone that can show them the right thing to do. They just hear their buddies doing it, they go out and they buy a home, but they haven't done all the certification, they haven't verified that this property's not going to have termite issues or meth issues, or something else that could really hurt them. They think, "Oh, it's a good deal, I can buy that and make a ton of money." The benefit to real estate is there's tons of people and there's tons of organizations out there that have already done it a thousand times, so connect with them. Join an investment club, join a company that does education, and then they'll help you limit your potential risk.

Shannon:

How have your mentors in real estate investing helped you to navigate pitfalls?

Woody:

We don't know what we don't know, and every deal has a potential problem, and every deal tends to really have a problem. I'm in the middle of a transaction right now where the home had to be lifted. We knew that there were some cracks in the foundation, but we weren't sure; so before we actually took ownership and before we actually even wrote the contract, we had an engineer come out. The only reason I did that is my mentor recommended, "You know what Woody, if you've got cracks in your foundation that are larger than average, hire an engineer. Spend the six, seven, eight hundred dollars. You'll save hundreds of thousands of dollars of potential losses for a small investment", so we did that and it ended up costing the seller $75,000 to raise that foundation. Had we bought that home not knowing that, we'd be out $75,000, so an $800 investment saved me $75,000.

Now, after the home was raised, we paid another $400 for an inspector to go out and verify absolutely everything. What he did is he pulled off all of the insulation in the basement and found another crack that we didn't know about, so now we're having another company come out and verify that crack because you can see daylight through the foundation. That's never good. You never want to see daylight in the foundation.

They're coming out to fix that. Once again, the seller will have to pay that and we won't.

Shannon:

How do you help other people learn more about real estate?

Woody:

Everybody has that friend who is in real estate. I'm that friend for my friends, and they will always ask me, "Woody what about this?" Or, "What about that transaction? What about that home you flipped?" What I like to do is just invite them to come along and take a look.

There's times where I'll take five of my friends and show them a house that I'm doing, show them the pitfalls and mistakes, and where's the benefit to changing it.

This one home, there is about $100,000 in equity from us just buying it right. I believe that when it comes to real estate, you make your money when you buy it, not when you sell it, so you have to buy it right.

Shannon:
You are obviously passionate about real estate. What actually inspired you to get into the industry?

Woody:
I grew up with my folks in a different generation where my dad was the traditional father who would always work and my mother would stay home. In the 80's when the market crashed and we didn't have a lot of money, it was a challenge, and so my mom became a realtor. She would list homes, so when I was very young, I'd go with my mom when she would go list a home. I'd walk through these homes and they were, to a kid, like a jungle gym. They were just so fascinating, and I grew up being exposed to real estate. I met some of the investors who my mom was selling for and it changed my life forever.

If you list a home as a typical realtor, you'll make 3 percent. The investor can make 10 to 20 percent. They're just taking the greater risk. The realtor doesn't have any risk. They have some advertising costs, but that's not a huge risk. The investor who bought the home, fixed it up, put new paint/carpet in, now is making $50,000, $100,000, $150,000 on a transaction. That blew my mind, and that was the second I knew I wanted to be in real estate.

Shannon:
What are some of the creative ways that you use now, or what is your favorite way to find a property to acquire a fix and flip?

Woody:
For me the best way to find property is to know your area, so back to location, location, location. The home that I'm buying right now, the

one that had the sunken basement, we've been trying for two years to get this home. We've talked to the seller, he wouldn't sell it to us. Then low and behold we found out that he passed away, and then we went to his heirs, which was his older sister. Well, she's eighty-four years old. She doesn't want to deal with this property. She lives out of state, but because I was driving around, just driving by this one house that I've always wanted to acquire, I saw a car there. I knew he lived out of state. It was an investment property for him, so when I saw a car there, I just knocked on the door. And told them that because the home had been vacant for over three years, that's why it was neglected and the home sunk. Basically, I was able to get the home before it even went on the market.

Had they taken the time to invest in the property, to fix it up, and then to sell it, I would've been out of the loop. So to me the best technique is, take an area, a geographical area that you know well and trust, and then master it. Know every house. You can pull titles. You can find out when people are delinquent. You can ask them to buy the home before it goes into foreclosure. There are so many techniques to save yourself time because it's trying to find that jewel in the rough. It's always hard to find, but when you find one, you can pull out fifty to a hundred grand.

Shannon:
How do you decide if you are going to fix and flip a home or buy and hold it for rental income?

Woody:
If I'm in a financial position where I can hold it and I can keep it long-term and I believe a certain area geographically is going to go up in value, then I will hold it. I have done holds in the past, but on the fix and flips, those are the ones that give you large pops. Wealthy people, I believe, get wealthy by the large pops–fifty grand, a hundred grand, two hundred and fifty grand pops. I've made $200,000 on a house in thirty days. I can't save that much money myself, I can't save my way to wealth, and I don't believe most people can. You look at CEOs who have large stock options and a buyout takes place; they

get a large pop of millions of dollars, so to create massive wealth, you've got to have large pops.

Well, as soon as you've had enough large pops where you've got a good nest egg, now you can afford to buy one, hold it, and if a renter does not pay, you can afford to make that monthly payment. I don't believe in being house poor. If you own a bunch of properties but you can't fix up the yard or you can't take a vacation, I call that being house poor. You may have a million dollars in real estate, but you can't afford to take a vacation, then you don't have the life that real estate's designed to give you.

Shannon:
I'd like to go back to when you said you saw the car and you just knocked on the door. Tell me how that conversation went?

Woody:
It's very simple. You can tell when somebody is stressed. You can see it on their face. This woman looked bewildered. This is the first time she had seen this home after her brother passed. She didn't want that property. She lives two thousand miles away. She wants nothing to do with this property. I asked her, "You know what, I've been watching this home for two years. Are you the new owner? She said, "Yeah, my brother passed, and now I have inherited this home." I said, "Well, what is your intention? Do you want to sell the home, or do you want to keep it and rent it out? What would you like to do?" "Oh my gosh, I just want to sell this home," she replied, so I gave her an offer on the spot. She turned it down. I waited about a month. I kept checking on the home. I saw them doing yard work trying to fix it up. I went back to her, I said, "You know what, are you by chance interested in selling the home yet?" At that point, she was, because she just realized how much work it was going to be to fix it up.

You have to understand that if someone is going to sell you a house at a discount than what it should be going for, that means there's inherently something wrong with the home. Either it needs new carpet, or they had pets in there, or it smells. It's been neglected. Things are broken. So when you're looking for a fix and flip, they're never in perfect condition, otherwise they'd get top of the retail value. People who have these homes don't want them because they know how much it's going to cost to fix it, and that was the case with her, so it was really easy to buy it from her, to take that pressure and stress off of her.

Shannon:

Do you think that you can have real estate success being a one- man-show, or do you think that most people need to have a team?

Woody:

When I say I'm a one-man show I don't want to imply that I don't have a team and I don't work with other people because that's not true. I don't have employees that I pay that help me run my company, but I have a network of people that I work with. In real estate you cannot be successful without a network of people. It's impossible. You need to know a title guy, a realtor. You need to know an appraiser. There are so many moving parts in real estate, you need to have a group of people you work with.

When it comes to education, I go back to that saying, "We don't know what we don't know." Create an environment and a network, facilitate a mastermind, put people who are in real estate in the same room and you will expedite your knowledge. You'll expedite your learning curves. It is crucial that you spend time with a team of people who have your best interest in mind to make you successful.

Shannon:

What is your favorite investment strategy when the market is good and homes are selling quickly?

Woody:

In California in 2005 when the market was just exploding and homes were appreciating at 30 percent a year, if you bought a home for $400,000, in a year it was going for a $520,000, so in that market we were buying homes that weren't even built yet. When a new subdivision was under construction we would put down $5,000. Homes would take six months to nine months to build. By the time we bought that home and moved into it, we already had $60,000 to $80,000 of appreciation; so in an up market my favorite thing to do is speculation. Know an area, know where the parks and schools are being built, buy homes that are under construction so that you can flip them as soon as you close on them.

Shannon:

When you look at everything that you do in your life, your real estate investing career, your entrepreneurial adventures, and your life married with children, what legacy do you want to leave?

Woody:

I want my children and the people that I have the opportunity to come in contact with to realize that they can change. Regardless of your past, regardless of where you started, you can change. I believe real estate is one of the greatest agents for change. It allows someone, even an uneducated person like myself, to learn something, to master something, and then to make a very good income with it.

My legacy is that I want people to realize they can do it. That's the bottom line, that they can have their own life, that they can change, that they can become who they want to become regardless of their background.

As my wife would say, "We are just borrowing it for a time before the next generation borrows it." Since we don't take anything with us, I would want my legacy to be the impact I have had on my relationships. There is no doubt my life has been better because of the lives of others. I would like to do the same for someone else.